ONE JOURNEY
ONE NATION

God Bless you Benjamin,

Dennis Balcombe

包德宁

30-6-2018

ONE JOURNEY ONE NATION

AUTOBIOGRAPHY OF

DENNIS BALCOMBE

MISSIONARY TO CHINA

Generation Culture Transformation
Specializing in publishing for generation culture change

eGenCo. LLC
824 Tallow Hill Road
Chambersburg, PA 17202 USA
Phone: 717-461-3436
email: info@egenco.com
Website: www.egenco.com
            www.egenbooks.com

facebook.com/egenbooks
twitter.com/vishaljets
youtube.com/egenpub
egenco.com/blog

Paperbook ISBN 978-1-936554-04-1
ebook ISBN 978-1-936554-05-8

First Printing: 2011

Cover Design by Ambert Rodriguez, www.guezworks.com
Cover Photograph Selena Jetnarayan, www.posephotoco.com
Text Design and Typesetting by Kevin Lepp, www.kmlstudio.com

*I dedicate this book to the members of
the body of Christ worldwide, who have
supported the ministry in China in prayer
and finances. The distribution of bibles to the
Chinese church is made possible because of you.*

ENDORSEMENTS

It has been my pleasure to know Dennis Balcombe for 40 years as a personal friend and co-laborer in the Gospel. I remember when he said he had been "called" to China—at a time when the Bamboo Curtain forbade any missionaries to enter. Many people felt it was an unrealistic dream at the time, but Dennis knew he had heard from God.

How proud we are of the work that has been accomplished in China through his persistency. In the decades to come, this man will go down in history as the one who touched "the soul" of a nation.

—Dick Iverson, Founder
City Bible Church
and
Ministers Fellowship International

Rapidly emerging as a global superpower, China is now challenging the rest of the world to learn more about its culture, language, and socio-economic potentials. In this book, Pastor Dennis Balcombe gives a vivid account of how China has also become the world's largest and most important mission field, mingling his own experiences and the current situation in China.

My secretaries keep me updated on worldwide mission works by providing a constant flow of books and reports regarding various mission fields. Few of those materials describe the missionary work primarily as an initiative of the Holy Spirit as this book does. Reading *One Journey—One Nation*, I was so deeply moved and touched on how meticulously, as well as miraculously, the Holy Spirit has trained Pastor Balcombe for the Chinese mission. The author's report of how the Holy Spirit established a church in Hong Kong as a missionary outpost to China captured me so much that I thought I was with him in the mission field. I am confident that readers of this book will have the same experiences as mine.

After reading this book, one might even want to proclaim that the Holy Spirit is writing another chapter of the Book of Acts in modern China! I would greatly recommend this book for those who are interested in the works of the Holy Spirit, for those who are praying for the Chinese mission, and most of all, for those who are anticipating a change in life through the power of the Holy Spirit.

—Pastor Yonggi Cho, Senior Emeritus
Yoido Full Gospel Church
Seoul, Korea

Dennis Balcombe is a modern-day "Apostle Paul" in spirit, heart, faith, and dedication. Dennis has put his life on the line in order to preach Christ in China and to raise up thousands of leaders. He has inspired the Church worldwide with his humility and love for the nations. A rare gift to the Church, this man has given us his own treasure—a story of his life and journey. We honor you, Dennis, for a life well-lived for Jesus.

—Dr. Frank Damazio
Lead Pastor, City Bible Church
Chairman, Ministers Fellowship International

Pastor Dennis and Kathy are some of our dearest missionary heroes. They were the first ones to welcome us into Hong Kong and bless us with our visas. Their passion for China missions is contagious. They are people who have paid the cost and laid down their lives to bring the lost home to the Lord. Their holy-given lives have truly impacted a nation, and their stories must be heard. It is a joy to call Dennis and Kathy our friends.

—Rolland and Heidi Baker
Founding Directors, Iris Ministries

For over 40 years we have been personal eyewitnesses to the ministry of missionaries extraordinaire, Pastors Dennis and Kathy Balcombe, whom God has sovereignly used to lay the groundwork for potentially one of the greatest harvests in the history of Christianity. As visionary pioneers, they mastered the languages, embraced the culture, and came to fully identify with the Chinese people for whom they have sacrificially given their whole lives. This book is a must-read for those who are contending for the transformational ministry in the nations.

—Dr. Violet Kiteley, Founder of Shiloh Church
and
Dr. David and Marilyn Kiteley, Shiloh Church

Dennis Balcombe's commitment to bring the Gospel to China has left a lasting spiritual legacy. In his autobiography, *One Journey—One Nation*, you will experience his personal journey in a story that will both challenge and inspire.

—M. G. "Pat" Robertson
Chairman of the Board
The Christian Broadcasting Network, Inc.

I am certain that this testimony of Pastor Dennis Balcombe will become the most cherished account to those who care for the Chinese churches and the development of God's Kingdom in China.

Dennis was the first white pastor I had met in my life. My prayer had been, "Lord, please send us preachers who dare to die for You, that we may be inspired." Yes, he did come; he has come with a vision from Heaven. His love for the Chinese souls is like a river of the Spirit. He is an upright man, an apostle with a heart of compassion and the love of a shepherd. Among the missionaries to China in the last 200 years, apart from Robert Morrison, Hudson Taylor, and the Christian martyrs, few are comparable to the Dennis Balcombe family in their love for and influence on the Chinese churches. The Balcombes have indeed offered their bodies as living sacrifices for Jesus. I am convinced that Pastor Dennis' personal testimony and his prophetic messages have given the next generation of followers of Jesus a model to imitate. He is changing our attitude toward ministry to God. Pastor Dennis Balcombe is one of God's servants who I respect and love.

—**Brother Yun, The Heavenly Man**
Chinese House Church

It was over 40 years ago that I was privileged to stand with Dennis Balcombe on the very threshold of his odyssey into China. From his cramped little room in Hong Kong, he shared his vision and his prophetic call to reach the people of China. His passion was contagious and his faith unwavering as he waited for the door to open. Soon it was both my pleasure and our son's (Marcus) to travel with Dennis and his teams to many parts of the interior of China. *One Journey—One Nation* is a heart-gripping account of God watching over His word to perform it! As we continue to travel into China, the present statistics bear out the proof that there are more Spirit-filled believers in China now than any other nation in the world. Dennis is truly God's apostle to China, and China is now destined to be a blessing by sending missionaries to all nations, expanding the Kingdom of our Lord Jesus Christ. I urge you to join this journey and help finish the task.

—**Moses Vegh**
Ambassador, Hope to the Nations
Board Member, RCMI

I have often said that Dennis Balcombe is the Hudson Taylor of our day, and so it is fitting that he tells his story so that future generations can know about this incredible 21st-century missionary. The amazing story of his life is conveyed throughout the pages of *One Journey—One Nation*, and my prayer is that it ignites the hearts of those who read it. There are no limits to what God can do with a surrendered life. This is what we see as this most remarkable missionary grabs hold of the call of God and, with faith, courage, and determination, sets out on a journey that does, indeed, empower a nation with the Gospel of Christ.

—Bishop Bart Pierce, Senior Pastor
Rock City Church
Baltimore, Maryland

Dennis Balcombe will be recognized both in Heaven and in history as one of the greatest apostolic voices to have ever impacted the great land of China. For over 40 years, Dennis and his wife, Kathy, have pioneered perhaps the greatest move of God by the Holy Spirit amongst the people of China. Without question, every great leader in every fresh move of God stands on the shoulders of the previous generation. At the same time, the anointing of necessity has to be transferred by the Holy Spirit Himself to each successive generation. The lives of Dennis and Kathy read like the Book of Acts. Clearly the Holy Spirit has raised them up to carve out an apostolic base in Hong Kong, from which to launch a major thrust into mainland China, amidst the threat of death, imprisonment, and constant danger. The fruit of their labors will live long after they have gone home to their reward, and the landscape of China will have been forever changed for the Gospel of the Kingdom's sake because of these valiant warriors. What you hold in your hand is a tome that contains both inspiration and revelation. *One Journey—One Nation* will change your understanding of what God can do when you make room for Him to do it. Let Dennis and Kathy's lives be an open book as you read the history-making, epic journey that you now are in possession of, and may it cause you to respond in an even greater way to the call of Christ on your own life.

—Dr. Mark J. Chironna
The Master's Touch International Church
Mark Chironna Ministries
Orlando, Florida

Many people can read history, but only a few make history. In his book, *One Journey—One Nation*, Dennis Balcombe shares a very basic, simple, and doable kind of obedience to God that leads to experiencing a supernatural and tangible manifestation of God's power. Some people write books focusing on the theory, while this book is backed up by the life testimony of a man who encounters God on a daily basis over a period of 40 years. He is a dedicated and focused man who is willing to pay the price for the sake of the Gospel.

Humble beginning and humble still—that's Dennis Balcombe.

—Paul Tan
President, Indonesian Relief Fund
Apostle, City Blessing Churches

I first met Dennis Balcombe at Shiloh Church some 40-plus years ago, and also met Kathy—before they were married. As soon as I heard of his autobiography, *One Journey—One Nation*, soon to be released, I thought, "It's about time!" This book is a must for the missions section in any leader's library. Page after page is packed with an unsung "miracle of China" under the ministries of the Balcombes. They are missionaries indeed, sent out from their "Antioch church"—Shiloh, and have certainly "hit the mark" for the will of God in the great nation of China! May God bless this book to the Body of Christ.

—Kevin J. Conner
Melbourne, Australia

I have placed before you an open door that no one can shut
...and you will be my witnesses...to the ends of the earth.
(Revelation 3:8b; Acts 1:8b NIV)

TABLE OF CONTENTS

Foreword   i

Prologue   iii

PART ONE

CHAPTER One   *Born for China*   1

CHAPTER Two   *A Form of Godliness*   11

CHAPTER Three   *Converted and Called*   23

CHAPTER Four   *Baptized in the Spirit*   35

CHAPTER Five   *Preacher in Training*   47

CHAPTER Six   *Holy Spirit Power*   61

CHAPTER Seven   *Fighting for Jesus*   77

PART TWO

CHAPTER Eight   *Becoming Chinese*   97

CHAPTER Nine   *Invading the Devil's Territory*   107

CHAPTER Ten   *Whirlwind Wedding*   119

CHAPTER Eleven   *Shockwaves*   131

CHAPTER Twelve   *Growth and Opposition*   143

CHAPTER Thirteen   *Fields White Unto Harvest*   155

CHAPTER Fourteen   *Why China?*   163

FOREWORD

God has allowed me the honor and privilege to travel the world, meet some of the greatest leaders in His Church today, and sit at their feet listening to the stories of God's supernatural activity in their midst. Along with the testimonies of Rolland and Heidi Baker in Mozambique, David Hogan in Mexico, and SoPhal Ung in Cambodia, Dennis Balcombe's autobiography is one of the most amazing stories I have ever heard. He has been used of God to touch leaders, evangelize the masses, and prophesy to people in a way that has radically changed their lives.

As soon as Dennis sent me the first three chapters of this book, I quickly devoured them, couldn't wait to receive more, and was extremely honored to have been asked to write the Foreword. This is the kind of book that introduces you to another dimension of a truly spiritual reality. It is full of the amazing ways God intervenes in our personal lives and in a nation's history.

On my first trip to mainland China, I traveled with a Chinese pastor who had arranged for me to meet the seven top leaders of one of the main underground house church movements in the nation. As I was interviewing them, I was told that these seven had led people to Christ, who in turn had led others to Christ, eventually forming a network of relationships and underground churches consisting of 25 million believers. Although they had begun evangelizing around 1970, about 80 percent of the 25 million had come to Christ only since 1988. I asked them what had happened in 1988. Their response— "Dennis Balcombe came to us and brought us the Holy Spirit."

I learned that Dennis had not only influenced this group but other underground church networks as well. Millions of people had come to Christ because of the profound influence of this one man's prayers and prophecies.

Later, I personally met Dennis and had the occasion to interview him at length. Eventually, he would come to speak at our conferences and at our local Global School of Supernatural Ministry. In my opinion, he is one of the great servant leaders, sent by God to fulfill his prophetic destiny and shake a nation with the Gospel. Dennis is an apostle, and his story is of a life laid down for the Master, Jesus, in China.

The stories of Dennis and his wife, Kathy, are not that of super Christians, but that of normal people, facing everyday problems and becoming victorious through steadfast obedience and faith. Yet this book allows us to peek into the world of "supernatural Christianity," the kind revealed in the Book of Acts. Your faith will definitely be strengthened in the power and leadership of God. I eagerly await the sequels.

—Randy Clark, Founder
Apostolic Network of Global Awakening
Author, There Is More

PROLOGUE

As I stepped from the plane onto the tarmac, a heady sense of anticipation swept over me.

Hong Kong!

Long had I looked forward to this day, the day I would first stand on the soil of the land to which God had called me years ago. I had been 16 then, that Fall of 1961, when I had given my life to the Lord, surrendered to His call to preach the Gospel, and received the baptism of the Holy Spirit. Almost on the heels of these experiences came His call to missions. "I want you to go to China," the Lord told me, a call that was quickly confirmed by the prophetic words of church leaders I knew and respected.

Now, nearly six years later, my feet were planted on the ground of China…well, Hong Kong, at least, which at that time was still a British protectorate, although the route I had taken to get there was different from what I had expected. It was 1967 and the Vietnam War was in full swing. The year before, I had been drafted into the US Army, unexpectedly, at the age of 21. Following boot camp I had been assigned to the infantry as a cook, and six months into my two-year time of service, I had been posted to Vietnam for a year. In the midst of my Vietnam tour, like every other soldier who survived long enough, I was granted a ten-day leave for R & R—rest and recreation.

The Army paid to fly me to my choice of five destinations—Bangkok, Taipei, Tokyo, Hawaii, or Hong Kong, where I then had ten days to spend at my leisure, doing whatever I wanted to do and could afford to do. So here I was, in Hong Kong.

I stretched a bit to ease muscles aching from hours of sitting during the bumpy flight over the South China Sea. The military transport wasn't the most comfortable ride in the world, but at least it was free. With duffel bag in hand, I headed into the terminal of the Kai Tak Airport, or, as it was known officially, the Hong Kong International Airport.

Given my missionary calling to China, my choice of Hong Kong for R & R had been a natural one. I had always been eager for any opportunity to be around Chinese people. Even back in the States, before my Army service, I had made several trips from my home in Long Beach, California to LA's Chinatown so I could share the Gospel there. God had given me a heart for China and the Chinese people, so being in Hong Kong just "felt right." It was where I belonged.

I certainly wanted to meet and mingle with the Chinese residents of Hong Kong, but I also had other, just-as-immediate desires—two in particular. First, I wanted to get away from the stress of the war. For weeks on end, I had been subjected to artillery and mortar rounds, machine gun and other small arms fire almost every day. People were dying. Soldiers on both sides were killing and being killed. The air reeked with the smell of gunpowder, napalm, chemical defoliants, and…blood. My calling was to preach life, not deal with death. I had longed to get away from that environment, even for just a few days.

Second, I was desperate for a hot bath or shower. In the field, water for bathing was a scarce commodity, especially for the infantry, because we were always moving from place to place. We had to grab any opportunity that came along, and it didn't come often. If we happened to come to a river, we would bathe if we had time. Sometimes, especially during monsoon season, a downpour of heavy rain would come, and we would strip off our clothes and grab a bar of soap. It was all we had. So the first item on my agenda after reaching my hotel was to take a bath.

Paul Collins, who I had met in Long Beach a couple of years earlier, was another reason I was in Hong Kong. Paul had been involved in the "restoration" movement of God that was big in the 1960s, and now lived in Hong Kong, where he worked with an organization called World Outreach (Asian Outreach today). Learning of my interest in and call to China, he once said to me, "If you ever come to Hong Kong, let me know and we'll get together."

So, when the time for my leave approached, I wrote to him and advised him of the dates when I would be in Hong Kong. But by the time I left for Hong Kong, I had not yet received a response from him, which I assumed could have been for any number of reasons. He could have been busy, and it simply slipped his mind. His response (or even my original letter) might have gotten lost or delayed in the mail, an easy thing to happen with the international postal service. He might not have learned I was coming to Hong Kong, and even if he had, he might have assumed I would be staying on a military base rather than in the field. I had no way to be sure that he knew I was in Hong Kong, and no other way of contacting him, or he me. This was before the days of cell phones and the Internet. So here I was in Hong Kong, wanting to find Paul Collins, but with no idea how to hook up with him. Trusting God to bring us together somehow, I prayed, "Lord, please help me connect with this man." If it was to happen, He would have to accomplish it.

As I settled into the back seat of the taxi that was transporting me from the airport to my hotel in Kowloon City, I gazed out the open window, soaking in the sights and sounds. It was quite warm, as it usually is there. The taxi whipped through streets filled with vehicles of every description—buses, other taxis, commercial trucks, government vehicles, private vehicles, motorcycles, motorbikes, and bicycles. Everywhere I looked, high-rise structures cluttered the skyline—hotels, office buildings, and apartment complexes. Then there were the people. Hong Kong is one of the most densely populated areas in the world. At that time, in 1967, the population was about four million; and to my eager, wondering eyes, they all seemed to be out on the streets and sidewalks. There were people everywhere.

The bustling life of this great city overwhelmed my senses—the blare of car horns, the grinding and growling of vehicle engines, the whine of motorbikes, and the delightfully musical lilt of spoken Cantonese. The air was thick with the acrid smell of gasoline and diesel exhaust. My first impression of Hong Kong was that of a wonderful city full of wonderful people who were vibrantly and vitally alive.

And most of them needed Jesus.

Then, just as quickly, as my taxi turned onto Nathan Road, the main north-south thoroughfare through Kowloon City, I saw a different Hong Kong—a darker view. Up ahead, rioters by the hundreds were smashing windows, fighting in the streets, and clashing with police, who had turned out in force in an effort to contain the violence. There was a lot of shouting, and even gunfire. What's going on? I wondered. Is this typical of Hong Kong?...This is just like Vietnam! That's when it began to dawn on me that I might not get as much rest here as I had originally intended.

I found out later what it was all about. The Cultural Revolution instigated by Mao Zedong and the infamous "Gang of Four" in mainland China had begun the year before. Strong resistance to these changes had brought China to the brink of civil war. There was rioting and fighting in the streets, and the Red Guards were fighting the Red Army. The violence and unrest bled across the border into Hong Kong. In fact, the local riots had been instigated by spies sent in from China, who used a recent rise in ferry fares as a pretext for protest. At one point, some Chinese soldiers actually rushed the border of the new Territories and penetrated a short distance into sovereign Hong Kong territory before they were stopped. For a while the whole situation was touch-and-go. There was widespread fear that China was about to invade and seize Hong Kong from the British, who had leased the colony in 1898 for a period of 99 years. The British-appointed governor of Hong Kong contacted Beijing and asked outright if the Chinese government intended to retake the colony. If so, he asked to be notified officially and to be granted a month's time to withdraw the thousands of British troops who were posted in Hong Kong. Great Britain was not prepared to go to war with China's one million-plus army. However, Beijing advised him that they had their hands full dealing with the civil unrest over the Cultural Revolution and had no intention of retaking Hong Kong. They instructed the governor to take whatever action necessary to keep Hong Kong free.

Shortly afterward, Hong Kong authorities cracked down. They knew who the riot instigators were—the communist agitators from mainland China—or at least how to get to their network. In the end, 50 people died in the riots. The instigators were arrested and sent back to China. The "official" response from the Chinese government was to arrest and deport some British diplomats. I, of course, knew nothing of this at the time, and neither did most of the residents of Hong Kong. No one could determine exactly how events would play out. The general assumption was that Hong Kong was about to be forcibly returned to Chinese control. That never happened, praise God. Disaster was averted, and the crisis soon passed. Hong Kong was still free...and has been ever since, even after reverting back to Chinese sovereignty in 1997, when Britain's 99-year lease expired.

Despite the rioting that day, however, I reached my hotel without incident. I located my room on the 18th floor, and it was there I discovered that my other immediate goal—a nice hot bath or shower—would not be achieved. There was no water. Hong Kong today has many reservoirs, and purchases tons of water from China...but it was different in 1967. At that time, Hong Kong was suffering a drought. There had been no rain for some time, so an emergency water rationing plan had been placed into effect. The water was turned on only every third day for three hours. Yet even that didn't help much, because by the time it reached my room on the 18th floor, the water pressure was so low it was practically nonexistent.

I couldn't escape the fighting, and I couldn't get a bath. Two strikes. So then I prayed to the Lord that somehow I would still be able to connect with Paul Collins before my R & R was up and I had to return to Vietnam. But how could one young American soldier on leave in a foreign city, who did not speak the language, hope to find one specific man among the teeming mass of four million inhabitants? I couldn't. Only God could pull that off.

Leaving the hotel, I took a cab to the waterfront and boarded the Star Ferry, which ran a daily two-way service between the Kowloon Peninsula and Hong Kong Island. Thousands of people made the ten-minute trip across Victoria Harbour every day. Recently, the fare had doubled, from five cents Hong Kong for downstairs and ten cents Hong Kong for upstairs, to ten cents downstairs and twenty cents upstairs, respectively. At today's rate of exchange, that would equate to about 1.2 cents US and 2.6 cents US. It wasn't a lot of money, but the rate increase was unpopular enough to become the flash point for the rioting that rocked the city while I was there.

As an American, I could easily have paid the higher fare for a place upstairs on the ferry, where both the seats and the view were nicer. But as a young soldier on leave, and having grown up in a family who never had much money, I knew the value of frugality. So, I paid the lower fare for a seat on the lower deck, which was almost full.

I sat down in one of the few remaining empty seats and observed the scene around me. There were men in sharp Western-style business suits reading newspapers; young mothers with small children in their arms; groups of young people, possibly students, chatting and laughing amongst themselves; young couples holding hands with eyes only for each other…. I was awash in a sea of Chinese faces, yellow skin, black hair, and dark eyes. I couldn't help but feel conspicuous, even though no one seemed to pay any mind to a blond-haired, blue-eyed American in their midst.

As I continued to gaze at the other passengers, I saw, from the corner of my eye, someone approach me. When I glanced up, to my utter amazement, there stood Paul Collins! The seat next to me "happened" to be empty, and Paul sat down right beside me. Now this was truly a miracle. He had not been specifically looking for me, yet among the four million in Hong Kong, he and I just happened to be on the same ferry at the same time, and he just happened to see me. And when Paul sat down, he didn't say something like, "Hello, Dennis, how are you?" or "Oh my goodness, I can't believe it's you." Instead, he immediately began to prophesy. It reminded me of the Old Testament prophet whom the Lord instructed, "Don't speak to anybody along the way, and do not have a meal with them; just give them My word."

"The situation in Hong Kong is very bad," Paul began. "Most of the churches have closed, and most of the pastors have left. Everyone assumes that Hong Kong is going to be lost. That is not going to happen. God is going to preserve Hong Kong. You need to come back as soon as you can, within a year, if at all possible, because you are going to start a church here in Hong Kong. One day China is going to open up, and when it does, you will be one of the first missionaries to go in." Having delivered the prophecy that God had laid on his heart, Paul then said, "How are you, Dennis? It's good to see you again. It's truly amazing that I found you."

There is no doubt in my mind that this was a divinely orchestrated encounter. Only God could have brought two specific people together so precisely, especially when one had an encouraging prophetic word for the other. And I was encouraged. I had come to Hong Kong for a little R & R, but God had another purpose in mind. The words Paul Collins spoke to me that day on the Star Ferry, words that God had placed in his heart, confirmed for me once again the call of God I had received six years earlier, when I was 16—the call to preach the Gospel in China, a call that was confirmed shortly after through the prophetic insight of others. Paul's word to me was just further confirmation that my call was sure and correct, and that God's destiny for me lay in China.

My leave in Hong Kong came to an end, and I returned to Vietnam to complete my tour of duty there.

But I knew I would be coming back.

PART 1

CHAPTER ONE

BORN FOR CHINA

*All the days ordained for me were written in your
book before one of them came to be.*
(Psalm 139:16b NIV)

I was born for China.

Even though I was born in Southern California, and spent most of my growing-up years there, my destiny lay in an ancient and exotic land halfway around the globe. And although God's call to take the Gospel to China did not come to me until the age of 16, the circumstances and experiences of my life from the very beginning helped to prepare me for that call. I lived on the West Coast of the United States for the first 24 years of my life, and the life lessons I learned during that time equipped me for life in Hong Kong, which has been my home now since 1969.

God never does anything in a haphazard fashion. He knows the end of a matter before it even comes into being. The psalmist said, "All the days ordained for me were written in your book before one of them came to be" (Ps. 139:16b NIV). Proverbs 16:9 (NIV) says, "In his heart a man plans his course, but the Lord determines his steps." Long before I ever took my first breath, God had a specific purpose for my life, and that purpose was China. He has a purpose for your life as well, and although it may or may not involve China, as mine did, it does involve something that only you can do. Not everyone is called to be a full-time missionary, but every follower of Christ is called to "make disciples." Jesus said, "Go and make disciples of all nations, baptizing them in the name of the Father and of the Son and of the Holy Spirit, and teaching them to obey everything I have commanded you" (Matt. 28:19-20a NIV). Don't imagine for a moment that you are too "ordinary" for such a purpose. I am one of the most ordinary people you could ever meet. God specializes in using ordinary people to accomplish His extraordinary purpose.

Looking back over my early years, it seems quite clear to me that God used even the most ordinary and mundane aspects of my life to prepare me for the work I was to do later in Hong Kong and mainland China. Even geography played a part. I was born in El Centro, California on April 3, 1945. El Centro lies east of San Diego, across the mountains, and is close to the Mexican border. Besides El Centro, where I lived until age five, and Washington State, where I lived from age five to age ten, I spent my childhood, teenage and young adult years in several other Southern California communities: Walnut, Pomona, El Monte, La Puente, and Long Beach, all of which are clustered in the vicinity of greater Los Angeles. This area of Southern California lies approximately 10 to 11 degrees latitude north of Hong Kong, close enough for the two regions to share a similar climate, although Hong Kong is about 700 miles closer to the equator. There are differences in climate, to be sure, but not nearly as many as if I had grown up in more northerly regions of the United States.

Even after I moved away from El Centro at the age of five, I returned to the community on several occasions to visit my grandparents, who lived there for many years. El Centro will always have a very special place in my memory, not only because it was my birthplace, but because it was where I received the baptism of the Holy Spirit. Summers were very hot there, and it was not uncommon for the daytime temperature to reach 120 degrees. I remember days growing up when, just for the fun of it, we would crack open a raw egg on the road, and watch it cook in about two minutes. The mountains to

2

the west blocked much of the moisture from the Pacific Ocean, so although it was hot, it was dry with low humidity.

Almost everyone had air-conditioning of some kind in their homes; it was a practical necessity. And fortunately, air conditioning was cheap in those days. The simplest set-up, found in even the poorest of homes, consisted of water flowing down through some kind of a filter with a straw in it, and an electric fan blowing on it. Anyone who had electricity and could afford a fan could have air-conditioning. Although primitive by today's standards, this system was quite common in those days…at least in my hometown.

Occasionally, we would drive southeast from El Centro to Mexicali, a city located right across the US-Mexico border. Mexicali is the capital city of the Mexican province of Baja California North. Directly across the border from Mexicali is the California town of Calexico. Today, Mexicali is by far the larger of the two, but in the late 1940s and early 1950s it was much smaller than it is now.

Interestingly enough, our main reason for going to Mexicali was usually for the Chinese food. Early in the 20th century, a land development company in California had employed thousands of Chinese laborers to develop the land in the northwest portion of the Baja Peninsula. After the work had been completed, many of those laborers stayed and settled in Mexicali. There were so many, in fact, that Mexicali had its own "Chinatown." At one time, in those early years, there were more Chinese than Mexicans in Mexicali.

Through the city ran the Rio Nuevo, or New River, which today is regarded as one of the most polluted rivers in North America. It was along the banks of the New River that I had been first exposed to true poverty. As we drove by, we would see people living right alongside the water, many of them in the shabbiest and most destitute of conditions you could imagine. We saw them washing their clothes in the river, drinking from the river, and even using the river for their bathroom. The extreme poverty of these people carved a deep impression on my young mind that has stayed with me all my life. Although I did not realize it until many years later, God was even then, at my young age, developing a missions mind-set and increasing my awareness of people and cultures beyond my own, and of the crushing poverty that defines daily life for so many of them.

I also witnessed human need firsthand on the American side of the border. My grandfather worked for the Veterans Administration, where his job was to help take care of the veterans in El Centro and the surrounding regions. This included locating hard-to-find veterans in order to deliver their monthly support checks from the government. On several occasions when I was older and living in LA County, I would return to El Centro for a visit, and my grandfather would take me with him on these excursions.

Many of the veterans lived in out-of-the-way places, well off the beaten path. Some were a little "off" mentally, while others simply did not want to be part of regular society. Quite often they lived like hermits. The federal government, nonetheless, was required to give them their allowance. And my grandfather's job was to find them. Hearing him talk of these men, and especially seeing them for myself on the occasions he took me with him, made a deep impression. I started to learn how to help down-and-out people who lived on the fringes of society. This too, I believe, was part of God's "training ground" for me in missions.

On one of these trips, we headed east into Nevada to find a man who had no real home, hence, no post office address. Although we made the trip on a paved two-lane road, my grandfather would point out parts of an old wooden plank road that ran parallel to the paved highway, and say, "That's the road I came to California on." He had arrived by wagon in the late 19th century, before there were any automobiles in the area or roads for them to drive on. My mother's grandmother was also one of the early pioneers to travel to California in a covered wagon. She even wrote a book about it. Although she died many years ago, I remember her quite well.

As my grandfather and I headed into the desert, heat waves from the baked roadway surface shimmered in the air in front of us. The day was long and tiring, but eventually my grandfather found the veteran recluse in a shack near the Boulder Dam and gave him his money.

My family has also always been very patriotic, and men in every generation have served their country in the military. My grandfather fought in World War I. My father fought in World War II, and was the only survivor when his bomber crashed on takeoff while setting out on a bombing mission over Germany. Some of my uncles served in the Korean War, and I served a one-year tour of duty in Vietnam with the U.S. Army. Because of this tradition of military service, veterans' affairs and organizations have played a significant role in the social activities of my family. I remember my parents or grandparents often attending a meeting or party or some other kind of veterans' get-together.

Growing up in a family who never had much money was also important in my preparation for missionary life, because I learned early on not to place a high priority on material possessions. Our family rarely purchased brand-name shoes, clothes, or other accessories. But whatever we lacked financially, we made up for in love. Our parents never had much, but they really loved us, took care of us, and did everything they could to support us, help us, and prepare us for success in life. I suspect that most people would rather have a loving and giving family, even with fewer material possessions, rather than to own everything money can buy and live in a family where love is absent.

I, along with my six younger siblings, learned generosity from our parents as well. We were a very compassionate and giving family who reached out to other people in need, even when we did not have a whole lot ourselves. Although we were not truly a "spiritual" family—we were "religious" Methodists with a form of godliness, but not the power (see 2 Tim. 3:5 NIV)—we always demonstrated a concern and care for other people.

Our parents gave us lots of love and lots of encouragement, and as a result, all seven of us children turned out quite well. Both of my brothers serve in the ministry, and all of my sisters have good families. Before she passed away several years ago, my mother was so happy in the knowledge that all three of her sons were preachers and were actively serving the Lord.

The parents I refer to are my mother and my stepfather, from whom I take my surname of Balcombe. I never was well-acquainted with my biological father because he and my mother had divorced when I was still very young. And being so young, I never really understood the reason for the breakup. After the divorce, I never had any additional contact with my biological father, and he since died many years ago. Thus, my stepfather is the man I have always thought of as my father. In fact, to me he has always been much more than a stepfather. So much of what I have learned to help me be successful in life—character, honor, honesty, and integrity—I have learned from him.

After my mother married my stepfather, we all moved to southern Washington State, because that was where his family lived. We settled in the small community of Cosmopolis, and later lived in the adjacent city of Aberdeen. Whereas California had been hot and dry, Washington was cold and wet, especially during the winter when it seemed to snow all the time. It snowed so often in the wintertime, in fact, that I remember many times when we could not go to school because the roads were closed—unheard of in Southern California!

My stepfather worked an irregular labor job, so most of the time there was not a lot of money. He was often employed painting tract houses that were being constructed in new housing developments. He also worked on different construction projects. To my knowledge, he never joined the labor union; consequently, without union membership, it was not easy to get those kinds of jobs. So he tended to migrate from one short-term job to another. Quite often, he would finish one job and go for weeks or even months before another one came along. Part of the problem was that it rained a lot in Washington; and when it rained, outside house painting and construction both had to stop. Even inside painting often could not be completed because the air was too damp for the paint to dry.

When we lived in Washington, our family owned a car. Although unable to afford a nice new car, my father did manage to acquire a Ford Model T from the 1920s, a car so old that it had no electric starter, but had to be hand-cranked. It couldn't go very fast, but it did get us around, and was the only car we had during the five years we lived there.

With a large family of four girls and three boys, our parents sometimes had trouble making ends meet. We moved frequently while living in Washington, either because we could no longer afford the rent, or because we simply wanted something cheaper. There were few times when we had no power or water because we had no money to pay the electric bill or water bill. That may sound sad, and at the time it was; yet there was a very positive side as well.

The scarcity of money taught us to be very frugal, a habit I have practiced all my life, and which has held me in good stead throughout the years of my ministry and mission work. So even in this, God's hand was present, preparing me, before I was even aware of it. I learned to work hard for every dollar; that it is very important to save money, that I should never buy anything that I cannot afford, and that I should never buy anything on credit.

And I learned those lessons well. To this day I have never had to pay a single cent in interest on a credit card. I never buy anything on credit, and I tell the people in our church never to buy anything on credit. That is the way I was brought up, and it has always worked for me. The bottom line: If you can't afford it, don't buy it. If I want to purchase a computer, for instance, I wait until I have enough money on hand to pay cash. Even when I bought my first car many years ago, I paid cash for it. The philosophy we were taught at home was, "Pay cash. Why pay good money to the bank?"

Many economists say that "cash and carry" is not a healthy way to manage a nation's economy, and that people as well as institutions need to borrow money in order to inject financial lifeblood into the economy. Whether or not this is true, no one can deny that debt is becoming an increasingly more serious problem at every level—personal, corporate, and national. Finances affect everything. It seems today that everyone is borrowing money. Many Christians, including many pastors, continue to increase their debt, only to discover that they can't pay it off. This causes not only financial problems and stress, but spiritual problems as well.

In our church in Hong Kong, we owe money to no one. Our

church building is completely paid. We never borrow money, because the Scripture says that "the borrower is servant to the lender" (Prov. 22:7b NIV). In addition, we advise our people not to lend money to anyone, nor be a guarantor for anyone. The Scripture likewise says, "Do not be a man who strikes hands in pledge or puts up security for debts; if you lack the means to pay, your very bed will be snatched from under you" (Prov. 22:26-27 NIV); and "Let no debt remain outstanding, except the continuing debt to love one another" (Rom. 13:8a NIV). Carrying personal debt or being a guarantor for another's debt can cause all kinds of problems. That's what I learned as a boy, and living by that principle has spared me many difficulties in my ministry over the years.

My parents' beliefs and values were simple and modest. The food we ate every day was plain fare, such as spaghetti, macaroni, beans, and the like. We seldom purchased expensive steaks or other meats. When shopping now, I never consider buying famous brand products when the non-brand or generic brand is just as good. Instead, I look for the cheapest item that will do the job, and when traveling I have no problem taking third class.

My parents did their best to provide for all of us, but we never acquired the nicer toys and items that others enjoyed. This too served me well, because it taught me to appreciate the little things, the simple pleasures of life. I learned to share with my siblings and my friends who were also middle or lower class. And still today, I am quite comfortable socializing with average or poor people. My brothers, sisters, and I also learned never to waste anything. Quite often, our clothes were hand-me-downs, and to this day I do not throw things away simply because they are old. If something is broken, I always try to repair it, if possible, rather than replace it.

Many of the old training books for missionaries, which predate today's prosperity mind-set, shared one common thread for mission-aries-to-be: "Expect to live a life of poverty." That was good counsel. Even though I was not aware of it at the time, God used all these experiences and materials to build in me a mind-set of simplicity, to teach me to be content and satisfied with the basics rather than crave an abundance of material things or the trappings of luxury.

One of my very earliest memories of Washington State involves my first real friend, and reveals again how God was already at work in my young life to prepare me for my call to mission work in China.

We had just moved to Cosmopolis, and when school started, I entered kindergarten at the age of five. One of my classmates was a Chinese boy whose family had recently emigrated from China to the United States. I do not know whether they came from mainland China or from Taiwan; at that age, I would not have known the difference anyway. I, of course, could not speak any Chinese, and he could speak only a few words of English; but we quickly became friends. I tried to teach him to speak English, and he taught me some Chinese words.

His family must have been fairly wealthy, because their house was much nicer than ours. In fact, compared to our modest cottage, their house was like a mansion. Everything about their house was Chinese. The furniture was Chinese; the pictures on the wall were Chinese; the house was filled with porcelain vases. I was utterly fascinated. The thing I remember most, however, was the expensive Chinese screen—a large partition made of a special kind of dark hardwood that lasts practically forever, covered with paintings, engravings, Chinese characters, and inlaid pearl and jewels—the kind of item that is found only in the homes of wealthy people.

Although my friend's English rapidly improved, neither of his parents or his grandmother who lived with them, learned to speak any English at all. Yet his grandmother, in particular, took an immediate liking to me.

My first introduction to another culture made a profound impression on me, and I instantly fell in love with China. My friend would talk to me about China, and I decided that it must be the most exciting place in the world. I wanted so much to learn Chinese from this family. And even more, I wanted to go to China! I was desperate to go! You know how children are—how they love to hear stories of faraway places and dream of visiting distant lands.

Because my mother had taught me to pray when I was three years old, I used to go to bed at night and pray that somehow I would be transported to China. I kept thinking over and over to myself, I know that I am going to be in China; I know that I am going to be in China! Then I would wake up in the morning and run to the window to see if I was in China. Imagine my disappointment when I discovered that I was not in China, but still in the town of Cosmopolis, Washington!

My Chinese friend was in school with me for only about a year, and then went away. I do not know whether he simply moved to a different school, or a different city, or if his family returned to China; but I never saw him again. A few years later, my family left Washington and returned to Southern California. Eventually, I forgot all about him. It was not until after the Lord called me to mission work in China at the age of 16 that I remembered that my first friend had been Chinese. It was as though God had had His hand upon me even at the age of five, and placed within me a love for China and the Chinese people. Through my friendship with a young Chinese boy, God had planted a seed in my heart that burst into bloom ten years later.

CHAPTER TWO
A FORM OF GODLINESS

Having a form of godliness but denying its power.
(2 Timothy 3:5a NIV)

Even though my stepfather's family also resided in the same Cosmopolis-Aberdeen area where we were living, things did not go as well for us as he had hoped. Consequently, after five years living in Washington, we moved back to Southern California. I was ten years old when we drove all the way from Washington to Los Angeles County in an old car from the 1930s or 1940s that my father had managed to buy.

And during this trip, high in the hills on the road leading from the San Fernando Valley to Los Angeles, our car broke down. I don't remember what the specific problem was, but it was something major, like the transmission or the clutch. Here we were, nine people—two adults and seven children—stranded on the side of a mountain road in Southern California. Simply finding someone to repair the car was difficult enough, but the fact that we had practically no money made it almost impossible. It was quite a hardship for us. We all had to sleep in the car for a few days before we got off that mountain. Yet at ten years of age, it was just another adventure to me. I felt like one of the early pioneers enduring all kinds of difficulties in their determination to reach the "promised land" of California. This was one more "life lesson" imprinted on my mind, teaching me to appreciate the more important things in life and never to take anything for granted.

For a short while we lived in the small community of Walnut, located between the cities of Pomona and El Monte. The name Walnut was derived from the abundant walnut groves that once had graced the area; but by the time we had moved there, the walnut groves were long gone. During the next eight years, until I left home for Bible college at the age of 18, we moved several times, living in Walnut, Pomona, and El Monte. Then, I graduated from Los Altos High School, which was near El Monte.

Living this close to Los Angeles made it quite easy for me to catch a bus to that great city and visit Chinatown. Once I had accepted my call to missions, I had a passionate desire to be among Chinese people. At that time, there were very few Chinese where we lived. Today, it is different. I returned to the area a few years ago and found that it is now almost all Chinese. In fact, there are more Chinese in that part of Los Angeles County than there are in Hong Kong. The area has become so transformed that in some parts you will find no English. The signs are Chinese, the stores are Chinese, the restaurants are Chinese…everything is Chinese. Immigrants from China can settle there and fit in immediately and feel almost as if they have never left home. They don't even have to be able to speak English.

After a short time living in Walnut, my father was able to buy a large but modest tract house in Pomona for $20,000, with no money down. It was just one of hundreds of almost identical tract houses that lined the highway between Los Angeles and Palmdale. The house came equipped with a washing machine, dryer, a heater, an air conditioner, and several other amenities. My parents did not have much money, so it was quite a blessing that they were able to purchase such a house. They lived there for many years, and I spent most of my adolescent and teenage years there.

In those days, Southern California was still developing, and the area where we lived was still fairly new and rather sparsely populated. Consequently, the nearest school was quite a distance away. My brothers, sisters, and I rode the bus to school, but we first had to walk to the bus stop. And that in itself was a long trek. We did not have the luxury of paved sidewalks, and the side of the road where we walked was no more than a dirt path studded with sharp rocks and lined with thorns and briars.

At the beginning of each school year, my father bought me a new pair of shoes. They were not name-brand, high-quality shoes, but a pair of the cheapest shoes on the market, which in those days cost about five dollars. They were supposed to last an entire year. However, due to the poor quality of the shoes and miles of walking every day, the soles of the shoes wore out after only a few months, with holes that exposed my socks to the ground. I tried to solve this problem by putting cardboard in the bottoms of my shoes. Unfortunately, the cardboard provided little protection from the thorns and sharp rocks on the road. By the time I arrived to school, or returned home, my feet were bloody from where they had been cut and scratched. Although quite painful, the cuts were fortunately never serious.

Unlike many of my friends and schoolmates, I was never interested in sports or any kind of athletics while growing up. I did enjoy music, and I played clarinet in the school band. But my real passion was science, particularly chemistry and physics. I also liked electronics and computers—anything high-tech—and I loved tinkering around with machines or anything mechanical. Blessed with an inquisitive mind, I always wanted to know why and how things worked and was anxious to figure out a way to make them work better.

One day when I was very young, not more than five or six, I decided to take apart an old family clock to find out how it worked. Using a screwdriver, I removed the back panel from the clock and gazed wonderingly at the busy array of organized springs, sprockets, gears, and flywheels. Immediately I began to dismantle the mechanism, certain within myself that I would remember where everything went when it was time to put it all back together.

Although I had a relatively good idea of how the clock worked, I ran into a little problem when I tried to reassemble it. Things were going along pretty smoothly until I got ready to put the back panel on and realized there were still five or six small parts still left on the table. Try as hard as I might, I could not figure out or remember where they went. As a result, that old clock never worked again.

Of course, my parents were not very happy that I had destroyed a perfectly good clock, but in the end, they were basically philosophical about it. In fact, when I was 13 and told my mother that I wanted to be a scientist, she was not surprised by my desire and reminded me of this clock incident and how much I loved to investigate things, even at a very young age.

With my natural curiosity and my love of tinkering and experimenting, I knew by the time I reached my teens that I wanted to become a scientist. Chemistry and physics fascinated me; and outside of school, scientific experiments consumed much of my spare time. At that point in my life, I was quite introverted. I cared nothing for sports, was not interested in girls, and never went to parties. Even during summer vacation, I took as many summer classes offered by the school as I possibly could. My hunger for knowledge was insatiable. I loved to study, I loved to read, and I loved to experiment. I guess you could say I was a classic science "geek" even before there was such a word.

Whatever little money I received from my father or earned from jobs here and there, I used to buy different chemicals to perform experiments at home. When I wasn't conducting experiments, I was reading about physics. I excelled in school, graduating 16th out of 3000 students in my high school class, not because I was exceptionally bright, but because I loved to study, believed in working hard, and always did my homework. Had it not been for God's call on my life to preach the Gospel and become a missionary to China, I have little doubt that today I would be a scientist. But I have no regrets passing up a scientific career since no life could ever be as satisfying and fulfilling, and no pursuit as significant, as the life I have spent bringing the message of the Good News of Jesus Christ and the baptism of the Holy Spirit to the Chinese people.

Due to my excellent grades, when I reached my third year in high school, I was placed in a special accelerated course of study in which two years of course material were compressed into one, so that by the time I graduated from high school I had already completed the equivalent of my first year in college. It was fortunate that I liked homework, because with all the accelerated classes, I had a lot of it. I learned very quickly that the only way I could complete all my homework was to get up very early every morning. Even at the age of 15 or 16, I was waking up at 4:00 a.m. to spend a few hours on my homework before school. After I found the Lord, I added an hour or two of prayer to my morning routine. At church we were encouraged to pray an hour every day, and that is what I did. If there was no prayer meeting at the church, I would go out to the mountains or hills beside my house and pray for an hour in the morning.

Consequently, I started the habit of sleeping only four or five hours a night, and that has been my practice ever since. It works well for me. In fact, if I sleep more than six hours, I get a headache, become very tired, and am no good to anyone. But if I sleep only four hours, I sleep very well and wake up completely refreshed. I also learned how to sleep anywhere, anytime, and under almost any conditions. Sitting up, lying down, in light or in darkness, in quiet surroundings or noisy—if I want to sleep, I can sleep. This has been extremely beneficial to me over the years, because by sleeping less each day, I get more accomplished. And considering my busy travel schedule, particularly in recent years, my ability to fall asleep under any circumstance—on a crowded airplane with babies crying, for example—has been a real asset.

Although my parents instilled in their children solid principles of character, honor, and integrity, and taught us high moral values, our family was only nominally religious. We were Methodists, but not really Christian in the truest spiritual sense of the word. My father seemed indifferent and sometimes even hostile to the idea of Christianity, or at least the Pentecostal brand of it. Surprisingly, his father was a Pentecostal preacher who we visited many times when we lived in Washington. When I, at the age of 16, told my father that I had become a Christian and had been called to be a preacher, he became very upset, not so much because I had become a Christian, but because I had become involved in a Pentecostal church. At that time in his life, my father was not serving the Lord, and I suppose that my conversion to Christ and call to preach reproved him, causing him to react in a negative manner. However, after I had left home and was serving in Vietnam, my father eventually grew to love the Lord.

My grandparents in Washington lived in a house right behind their church, which was located just off one of the main highways in the state. It was an old-style church, with a steeple, and a cross on top of the steeple. It was large enough to hold 100 to 200 people. This connection to the true Gospel and ministry of the Holy Spirit, although scanty, would deeply impress me as a young boy. I am also confident today that my grandparents spent much time in prayer for me, which undoubtedly was one major reason God saved me and called me into Christian ministry and missions.

Spiritual influence in my life began at a very young age through the efforts of my mother. Donna Joyce Balcombe was a very beautiful and godly woman who loved all seven of her children dearly. She compiled many scrapbooks of pictures, awards, certificates, letters, and other items relating to her children. To this day, I still have a pair of baby shoes she had "embalmed" and a newspaper article regarding a baby contest that I had won as the "cutest baby." I also have letters, and even a poem, which I had written to her while I was in Vietnam. She had framed them all.

My mother was quite a woman. After devoting her early years to being a full-time housewife and raising seven children, she then studied hard and obtained her license as a realtor. I don't think she ever made much money, but it was still quite an accomplishment to pass all those tests and earn that license. She also was an accomplished writer and published a book entitled, The Year of Janie's Diary, a fictional book about young people growing up and dealing with various family situations. At the time, it was acclaimed to be a very good book. She had based the characters in the book, at least in part, on what she had learned in raising her own children, although names and events were changed.

I was baptized when I was three weeks old, and I remember very specifically that I was praying by the time I was three years old. By the age of five, I was praying every night. My mother taught me to pray the Lord's Prayer and the Twenty-third Psalm; and just before bedtime, I always prayed the familiar prayer known to countless children for generations: "Now I lay me down to sleep, I pray the Lord my soul to keep. If I should die before I wake, I pray the Lord my soul to take."

In addition to teaching me to pray, my mother was a Sunday School teacher who took me and my brothers and sisters to Sunday School every week. She wanted us to learn the Bible, so my siblings and I established the habit of going to church at a very young age. My mother, grandmother, and great-grandmother were Methodists. In fact, several generations of my mother's family had been Methodists. We were quite religious, yet because of the spiritual deadness in the Methodist church that we attended, none of us really personally knew the Lord, with the exception of my mother.

While the Methodist Church claims a great and godly heritage, this heritage has been all but lost in many of its local congregations today. This is just one example that supports why it is so important that we continue to speak the truth and persist in preaching foundational beliefs so that the fires of revival burn in every generation.

John and Charles Wesley established the Methodist Church in the mid-18th century. Many people have expressed that had it not been for the ministry and spiritual awakening inspired and spearheaded by the Methodists such as the Wesleys, George Whitefield, and others, England would have suffered a bloody, disastrous revolution such as the one which had occurred in France. Instead of a violent uprising, however, England experienced a peaceful transition to a successful form of democracy, and during the next century also underwent significant social reform. The revival was so widespread that it changed the hearts of millions of people in England. It even crossed the Atlantic Ocean, where the preaching of George Whitefield ignited a spiritual flame in the hearts of thousands in the American colonies, and became a major force in the Great Awakening of the 1740s.

My grandmother on my mother's side was part of what they called the "shouting Methodists." She related to me that in those days, the Methodists preached holiness, prayer, and evangelism. At the front of the church was a bench that they called the "shouters' bench." Every service concluded with a clear altar call: "You must get saved; you must repent of your sins." If you were a sinner under conviction, they expected you to come forward, kneel down, pray, repent, cry, and become very emotional. To their way of thinking, unless they saw tears, you were not truly saved. They believed in prayer, the Bible, preaching Jesus and getting people saved.

But by my generation, everything had changed. Many Methodist churches, including the one I had grown up in, had completely lost that hunger for the Lord and evangelistic fervor that had once so characterized the Methodist denomination. Like many other mainline Protestant churches of the day, the Methodist Church by and large had embraced modern liberal theology, which had its beginnings in the latter part of the 19th century with the development of "higher criticism" in Germany. Higher criticism was an approach to studying and analyzing the Bible as simply another work of literature. This method denied miracles, supernaturalism, and divine inspiration, and regarded the Bible as a work of strictly human composition. As a result, the traditional view of the Bible as the Word of God was torn to shreds, and the Gospel message of salvation through Jesus Christ was devalued and almost lost. Even today, higher criticism and the liberal theology it spawned continue to eviscerate the Gospel and destroy the faith of many.

There were exceptions, of course. Then, as now, there were Methodist churches, such as the Free Methodists, and the Wesleyan Methodists, who never went down the liberal path, and to this day remain conservative and evangelical. Unfortunately, however, the Methodist church I attended as a boy was not one of those.

I remember, as a young man of 13 or 14 years of age, going to Sunday school but never actually being taught the Bible. On more than one occasion, I specifically recall the Sunday school teacher saying something like, "As you know, there are four Gospels, and these were written about 40 or 50 years after the time of Jesus. Now, can you remember what happened 30 years ago?" (None of us in the class were 30 years old yet, so of course we couldn't remember.) The teacher continued, "Nobody today can remember what happened 30 years ago, nor could they even in those days. Moreover, they had no tape recorder, or any other effective way of recording history. Obviously, then, when it came to writing the Gospels, they had to rely on memory, so there must be many mistakes. Inevitably, then, the Gospels have to be full of errors and inaccuracies." Rather than teaching the Bible, they were actually teaching unbelief.

Being exposed to this kind of teaching week after week, I could not help but be influenced by it. My faith in the Bible, in prayer, and even in the very existence of God was gradually whittled away during my boyhood years. Add to this the fact that I never saw any miracles, rarely experienced answers to prayer, and never sensed the presence of God in church, and it comes as no surprise that by the time I was a young teenager, I was, for all practical purposes, an agnostic. Although I was religious and a churchgoer, I saw no reality of God in church. It would not be until I was 16 that God would become real to me, and I would truly give my heart to Christ.

On Sunday mornings, when the pastor got up to preach, he would lecture about everything, except the Bible. He talked about politics and about society; he referred to reference books and magazines; he spoke about the latest medical advance. Basically, we were taught that we had to be good people and contribute to society, but we were never told, "You need to repent of your sins, place your faith in Jesus Christ as your Lord and Savior, and be born again."

The Sunday morning service was about an hour long, and I was always amazed that the pastor would, without fail, end exactly at 12 o'clock noon. In fact, you could set your watch by his promptness. When he said, "Amen," you could be sure that it was 12 o'clock on the dot, not one second before or after. Every part of the service was closely regimented and followed a rigid schedule—the singing, the prayers, the choir anthem, the sermon. Yet there was never an altar call. There was a designated time in the service, however, for prayer, probably hearkening back to my grandmother's day. During this time in the service, people could come forward to a bench at the front of the church and pray. But even this time was closely regulated.

I remember during one Sunday morning, I innocently made the mistake of walking up to the altar at the wrong time. I think it was during the time that the choir was supposed to sing. The result? I received a real tongue-lashing from the pastor. "What do you think you're doing? How dare you come and pray now? This is not the prayer time; this is the choir time. Didn't you read the bulletin?" I was so embarrassed and humiliated; all I wanted to do was pray. But in that church, you could pray only when they told you that you could pray.

It seemed to me that the reason many people went to that church was to meet and socialize with other people. There was little apparent genuine spiritual hunger. The young people were continually writing notes to one another while the pastor was preaching. And some people even used the time to pass out their business cards. I remember one man asserting, "I am a doctor at such-and-such a clinic. If you ever get sick and need help, come to my clinic, and I'll give you a special discount." Another man declared, "I'm a lawyer. If you want to divorce your wife, or if you have some other legal problem, look me up, and I'll help you out." Can you imagine—a lawyer drumming up divorce business in church? There really wasn't evidence of a hunger for God.

If you had asked me when I was 14 or 15, "Are you a Christian? Are you serving God?" I probably would have said, "Well, I tend to be more agnostic." I did not see any reality in the church. All I witnessed was hypocrisy. I would pray every day and would go to Sunday School every week, but I never heard the truth, nor did I see lives changed. All I noticed was a bunch of hypocrites. A couple more years of that and I probably would have left the church altogether. I was beginning to doubt that there even was a God. I had been praying all my life, but it seemed as though He had never done anything for me. And it was obvious that He had done nothing for anyone else. I was surrounded by empty ceremony; the sermons were totally boring and monotonous, and they had absolutely no relevance to my life or to what I wanted to do.

I am convinced that if I had stayed in that church, I would have been lost to this day. Yet although I could not see God, He saw me… and my life was about to be profoundly and eternally changed. As it happened, it came through the simple interest and concern of a neighbor.

ONE JOURNEY—ONE NATION

CHAPTER THREE
CONVERTED AND CALLED

Go into all the world and preach the good news to all creation.
… And these signs will accompany those who believe: In My name they
will drive out demons; they will speak in new tongues.
(Mark 16:15,17 NIV)

By the time I was 16 years old, my family was living in La Puente, California. As a naturally shy and bashful person, I wasn't very good at making friends and barely knew most of my neighbors. There was one person, though, who was both a neighbor and a friend—his name was Ron Coleman.

Ron lived right across the street from me and was a classmate of mine at Los Altos High School. He knew that I was a Methodist and went to church regularly. So, one day he asked me, "Do you see any miracles in your church?… In our church, miracles happen all the time."

"What do you mean?" I replied. "What kind of miracles?"

"People speak in other languages that they have never learned. Sick people are healed and sometimes demons are cast out of people."

Immediately, I began to argue with him. I may have been an agnostic, but my church had taught me well. The Methodist Church was the best church, and in fact, the only right church, even if we did hear more about John Wesley and current social issues than we did about Jesus Christ and the Bible.

"You are wrong," I exclaimed smugly, confident in my own superior knowledge. "Our minister says that miracles happened only in the Bible days; they don't happen today. You must be deceived."

Instead of arguing with me, Ron simply said, "Let me make a deal with you. I will come to your church, if you will come to mine. I don't want you to take my word for it; I want you to come and see for yourself. If what I am telling you is not true, then you don't have to believe it."

His suggestion sounded reasonable to me, so I agreed. Ron came to my church, and predictably, nothing happened. It was the same, usual dead Methodist service, full of formality and order, but completely empty of any sense of divine presence or supernatural power. Of course, I didn't recognize that at the time because I had never known anything different in church.

Now that Ron had fulfilled his part of the deal, I kept mine and agreed to go with him to his church. I didn't really know what to expect, and to be honest, after Ron's description of the "miracles" that took place there, I was a little nervous. I didn't want to see anything weird or experience anything crazy.

Ron's church was an Assembly of God church in El Monte, about an hour away. The moment we arrived, I could tell there was something different about this church compared to mine. First, the people met in a large house, because they had not yet built a church building. They were in the process of constructing one, but it would not be finished until about a year later.

Other differences became apparent as soon as we went inside. We had arrived in time for Sunday school, so we walked into a class for teenagers. It was a small room, filled with perhaps 20 guys and girls, most of who were close to my age. Everybody was talking informally and seemed to be having a good time. Maybe this won't be so bad after all, I thought as I sat down and began to relax a little bit.

As the class got underway, the teacher said, "Let us pray." I bowed my head and closed my eyes as I had been taught to do in my church.

The next moment I nearly jumped straight up out of my chair as everyone around me suddenly started praying out loud… and very loudly. Fear began to rise up inside me, especially when one big guy with a booming voice began shouting out words in a language I couldn't understand. These people are crazy! I thought. At that moment, I wanted more than anything else in the world to get up and run away, but I was literally too frightened to move.

As I sat there terrified, I noticed that many of the girls in the room were crying. Why are they crying? I asked myself. Is this a funeral? And if so, where's the casket? My fear began to subside somewhat as I paid more attention and realized they were telling Jesus how much they loved him. Their tears were of love, not sorrow.

I calmed down even more when I heard another teenage girl speaking what sounded to me like beautiful French. I had been taking French in high school for over a year, and although I could not make out exactly what she was saying, I knew she was speaking that language.

After Sunday School was finished, I went over to this young lady and asked her where she had learned to speak such perfect French. She looked at me with amazement and replied, "Did I speak in French? I had no idea."

The fact that she did not know what she had done made me even more curious. "Are you telling me then that you do not speak French?"

"That's right," she said.

"How do you explain it then?" I asked.

"I have never studied a foreign language," she told me. "I got married at 18 and never even finished high school." [She was 19 at the time.] What you heard was probably praying in tongues, a gift of the Holy Spirit."

I remembered that Ron had mentioned to me that they spoke in tongues at his church, but I hadn't understood what he had meant. I asked her to explain.

"When we are baptized in the Holy Spirit," she continued, "He gives us the ability to speak and pray in other languages. We pray in other tongues."

Although I did not realize the full significance of it until later on, this experience was a turning point for me. The foundation of my faith today is the work of the Holy Spirit. In everything I have done as a Christian—preaching the Gospel of Christ, and ministering among the Chinese—I have sought to honor the Holy Spirit, because I am convinced that the preaching of the Gospel of Christ, and the work of the Holy Spirit in power go hand in hand. This was true for the New Testament Church, and it is still true today. The Apostle Paul said,

When I came to you, brothers, I did not come with eloquence or superior wisdom as I proclaimed to you the testimony about God. For I resolved to know nothing while I was with you except Jesus Christ and Him crucified. I came to you in weakness and fear, and with much trembling. My message and my preaching were not with wise and persuasive words, but with a demonstration of the Spirit's power, so that your faith might not rest on men's wisdom, but on God's power (1 Corinthians 2:1-5 NIV, emphasis added).

Many people make a so-called "decision" or a commitment to serve the Lord merely by listening to an eloquent sermon. They are deeply moved emotionally by a wonderful "feel-good" religious service where they heard a great choir, a compelling altar call, and the comforting words of a trained counselor—even though they have seen no miracle. Later on, despite their so-called commitment to the Lord, they fall away when difficult times come, or when the enticements of the world draw them away. But someone who has seen a miracle knows that he or she has witnessed the supernatural, and the mind cannot deny it. In human terms, it is impossible. Either the Bible is true, or miracles are a work of the devil.

Hearing this young woman speak in perfect French, a language she had never studied, certainly convinced me that something unusual was going on, and made me curious about the worship service to follow. I was anxious to see what would happen next.

The worship service was held in the largest room of the house, which had been converted for church use, and was crowded with almost 200 people in attendance. Bill McKay, the pastor, and his wife, Marjorie, led the congregation in worship. Both of these wonderful servants of God, who have since passed on to glory, moved mightily in the works of the Holy Spirit, which I witnessed that morning.

I managed to find an empty seat next to a man who introduced himself to me as a "converted Jew," a Jew who becomes a follower of Jesus Christ and acknowledges Him as God's promised Messiah. Today, he and others like him are better known as Messianic Jews. As we chatted before the service began, I may have mentioned something about my experience in Sunday School where everyone was praying in tongues, because he asked me, "Would you like to see a miracle?"

"Yes, I would," I admitted.

"Then keep watching," my new acquaintance replied. "Sister Marjorie McKay often gives messages spoken in perfect Hebrew, and then translates what she has said into English. I know for a fact that she does not speak a word of Hebrew on her own; she has never studied it. I speak Hebrew fluently, however, and I can vouch for the accuracy of her messages. Let's see if she gives one today."

This church was typical of the old Pentecostals who usually spoke in tongues and interpretations in every meeting. And sure enough, at one point in the service, Marjorie McKay stood up and spoke a message to us in what to my ears sounded like a very beautiful and flowing language. I could not understand it, but my Jewish Christian acquaintance smiled and acknowledged, "She is speaking in fluent Hebrew without a single mistake."

Sister McKay followed up her Hebrew prophecy, with its interpretation in English. I turned to the man next to me and asked, "Is she correct?"

"Yes," he replied. "As usual, her interpretation is a summary of the message, rather than a word for word translation. This explains why sometimes long messages in tongues are followed by short interpretations, and vice versa."

I don't know if I had ever paid as close attention to any church service as I did to that one. Peculiar activities were happening all around me, the like of which I'd never seen before. In that same meeting they prayed for several people who claimed instant healing. (I also heard about certain others in the church who had been previously healed of cancers, blindness, and all kinds of other problems.) There was lively singing, clapping, tongues, loud prayer, intense preaching, and at the end, an altar call during which many people went forward for salvation, prayer, or for the baptism of the Holy Spirit. The entire meeting was electrified with the presence of God. I had never been to a church meeting like that in all my life.

I went home that day realizing that for the first time in my 16 years of life, I had finally seen true Christianity—Christianity as it was supposed to be—Christianity that was full of life and joy and purpose and divine power. Everyone in that crowded room had seemed so excited to be there. The whole atmosphere had been suffused with an undeniable sense of divine presence that I had never experienced before, and especially not in the church in which I had grown up. It was such an amazing and shocking experience that at first, I did not know what to make of it. I had been touched at a very deep level, yet at the same time was not sure I wanted to go back.

Then two days later as I was resting in bed I heard a voice say to me, "My son, I want you to be a preacher and go into full-time ministry." The voice was so clear, the closest it could have been to an audible voice without actually being one. And as clear as the voice was to me, I was also quite convinced as to whose voice it was. Even though I had grown up in a dead church that did not preach the Bible or lift up Jesus Christ, and even though I was not a disciple of the Lord, or even born again at that time, I was absolutely certain that it was God who was speaking.

His voice was so real and so clear to me that I immediately got out of bed and went outside. At that time, I had been sharing a room with two of my brothers, and on that particular night, my father, who was not saved at the time, was still watching television. So I went outside in order to be alone. I then began to reason why I could not be a preacher.

"Lord," I argued, "You have made a mistake. I cannot be a preacher. First of all, in order to become a minister, I would have to go to a theological college. That is very expensive, and our family is rather poor. I know they would never be able to support me in my religious training.

"Second, a minister must be a 'people person.' He must love people, enjoy meeting with people, and be very open and outgoing. I could never do that. I am an extremely backward and bashful person, more suited to books, study, science, and physics. Because I am so shy, I have no really close friends. I don't have the personality to be a minister.

"Third, I know that ministers do not make much money. I want to get a good-paying job to support not only myself, but also my parents and my brothers and sisters. I can do that if I become a scientist, but not if I become a minister. So, I plan to make science and physics my life profession. I promise to go to church, pray, believe in You, and follow You, but I want to pursue a scientific career. I hope, with Your help, to make some scientific discovery that will benefit all mankind."

After I finished giving Him all my excuses, He simply said, once again, "I want you to preach the Gospel full-time." I continued to debate with the Lord for quite a long time that night, but to no avail. My thoughtful, well-reasoned arguments did not seem to impress the Lord. Finally, I went back to bed. The next day, the same voice spoke to me again, saying the same words. And once again, I argued with the Lord. This went on almost every night for three months. The Lord would speak to me about being a preacher, and I would continue to list all the reasons why I could not do it.

Interestingly enough, during this time my friend Ron never invited me to go to church with him a second time. It was not until September 1961, three months after that first visit, that he approached me again and asked me to go. By that time, I was more than ready to do so. But had I known beforehand what would happen at church that morning, I might have felt differently.

After the one-hour drive to El Monte, we arrived at the church at 11:10 in the morning, ten minutes after the service had started. The church was packed, so Ron and his family and I squeezed onto the last row. Marjorie McKay, the pastor's wife, was already leading the worship. The congregation was halfway through singing a particular hymn when suddenly, she stopped. "There is no anointing in this song," she declared. "I do not sense the presence of God. Something is wrong. Let's sing another hymn." She then turned to another song in the hymnal.

This church was not like my Methodist church, where everything was written out in advance. In my church, we would sing whatever hymn was written in the bulletin, whether it was anointed or not. In this church, however, they chose songs that were suited to each particular service, even if it meant changing the order of the service on the spot. Their desire was to lead people into the presence of God.

After singing through only one stanza of the next hymn, however, she stopped again. "There is no problem with these hymns," she said. "The problem is that there is a young man here who three months ago had received a very clear call to the ministry. You have been rejecting that call for the last three months. But the Lord will not let you go. You know who you are, I know who you are, and you know I know who you are."

She was right. I knew she was talking about me. Suddenly, I found myself wishing I could hide under my chair or run out of the room. But there was no escape, and I knew it.

"I am not going to embarrass you," Sister McKay continued. "You must come forward of your own volition, repent, and give yourself to the Lord. If you do not come forward, the choir will not sing, the pastor will not preach, we will sing no more hymns, and we will not take up the offering. We will wait until you repent and respond to God's call. Do it now. Come forward and give your life to the Lord."

What else could I do? There was only one way she could have known about my three-month battle with God—He had given her a word of knowledge. And it was a specific word of knowledge. It was not a general word such as, "Someone has a headache," but a specific, detailed word that only God could have revealed. That was when I finally realized that I could not escape the call of God on my life. So I quit fighting. I said, "Lord, I give up. I will do what You tell me to do." I stood up and went to the front to pray.

The time was about 11:15 in the morning, and as soon as I went forward, the dam broke. The whole Sunday service became a prayer meeting that lasted until 1:30 in the afternoon. In all that time, the pastor never preached, the choir never sang, and the congregation did not sing any additional hymns. There were no announcements, and they never even took up an offering, which was like a miracle in itself for a church. What did happen, however, was that I gave my life to the Lord. I'm sure there were others whom God met in that service, because that church honored the Holy Spirit in everything. Maybe the pastor realized it was important simply to let me pray. Whatever the case, I prayed for nearly two hours, basically saying, "Lord, I will be a preacher, just as You have said, and I will follow You the rest of my life."

When it was all over, I got up knowing not only that I was saved and washed in the blood of Christ, but also that for the rest of my life, I would be a preacher of the Gospel. Thank God for churches that honor the Holy Spirit! Otherwise, I might never have ended up in the ministry.

But there is more. When I finished praying on that Sunday in October 1961, I knew that not only that I was saved and that I would spend my life preaching the Gospel, but I would also go and serve in another nation. In the spirit and inspiration of the moment, that seemed clear and self-evident to me. I needed no special revelation to understand that I would work out my call to ministry as a missionary in a foreign land. It was only logical, because the Gospel had already been spread all over America. Aside from the vast number of churches across the land, the Gospel was also available on radio and television, even in those early days of Christian broadcasting. Why would anyone who was called to preach the Good News stay in the United States? That seemed crazy to me. In my mind, it was perfectly obvious that I would be leaving my country.

So for me, the issue was not whether I should go to another nation, but which nation. I considered Africa, with its jungles, pygmies, elephants, zebras, and exciting safari adventures; but there was no witness in my spirit for Africa. I thought about India, but again, I received no witness. I considered other nations in Asia and South America, with the same result—I had no witness in my spirit for any of these places.

But about one month later, as I was preparing a report for school, I happened to open an encyclopedia to an article about China. Accompanying the article was a black and white picture of a Chinese boy. As I stared at the picture, I heard the Lord speak to me just as clearly as when He had called me to the ministry. "I am going to send you to Red China." In those days, we in America referred to mainland Communist China as "Red China." My call was very clear and specific—not Taiwan, or even Hong Kong, which I did not even know much about at the time, but mainland China. Given the political situation at that time, this idea was thought to be completely impossible.

First, the United States shared no diplomatic relations with China. The communists had closed the country after seizing power in 1947. Missionaries had to leave, Bibles were confiscated or burned, and churches were closed. As far as anyone in the West knew, there were no Christians left in China. Our only information was that China was a completely radical, atheistic, communist state. There was no tourism and no business connections to the outside. In almost every way, the Chinese people were cut off from the rest of the world.

In spite of all this, however, I knew beyond a shadow of a doubt that I had heard from the Lord—His call to me was clear and unmistakable. It was such a strong call, in fact, that at church the very next Sunday, I went to Marjorie McKay, the pastor's wife, and said, "God has called me to China. I'm going to go to Red China as a missionary."

Sister McKay could have easily laughed at me and told me I was crazy, but she did not. I have always been very grateful for that. Instead, she asked me, "How are you going to get there?"

"I don't know," I replied. "Can I walk? Is there a train?" I really had no idea. I had never flown in an airplane before, and didn't have any money. I had very little knowledge about the world in general. I was inexperienced, and it had never occurred to me that China was on another continent and that I had to get on an airplane or a ship in order to get there.

"Do you have any money for travel and living expenses?" Sister McKay asked.

"No, I don't have any money."

"Can you speak their language?"

For some reason, it had never occurred to me that Chinese people would speak Chinese rather than English. "No," I replied, "I don't know any Chinese." It was about this time that I remembered the little Chinese boy who had been my first friend when I lived in Washington State. I recalled that he did not speak much English, and I immediately realized that if I went to China and could not speak Chinese, I would not get very far.

Sister McKay continued to ask me practical questions that I had not considered. "Who is going to support you?"

I hadn't thought about that either. All I knew was that my call to China was very real, and I wanted to go. I had no other answers.

"What are you going to preach about?"

I hadn't been to Bible school…I didn't even know yet if I could preach.

It seemed like all her questions were aimed at convincing me why I should not or could not follow the call of God I felt on my life. That was not the case, however. Sensing, perhaps, that I was becoming discouraged, she continued, "I did not say this to you before, but the first time I saw you, the first time you visited this church, the Lord told me that you were going to be a preacher, and that you would go to China. I tell you this—China will open someday, there is no doubt about it; and when it does, you will be one of the first Western missionaries to go in. Don't be in a rush. You need to take time to prepare yourself, to study and to pray. Be patient. The day will come when you will go to China, but that time is not yet here."

Sister McKay's words encouraged me greatly. That is what personal prophecy is supposed to do—encourage and confirm what God has already laid on your heart. I learned early on to base my plans and actions on the call of God in my life, not on the prophecies I received, whether from Sister McKay, Paul Collins, or anyone else.

Prophecy is only confirmation; the call of God is what counts. There has to be something burning in your heart. As it turned out, China did open up, and I was one of the first Western missionaries to go in; but it was because of the call of God on my life, not the prophecies that were spoken over me. The prophecies merely confirmed what God had already planted in my spirit.

Even though at that time in 1961 China still lay several years before me, that did not mean I had nothing to do in the meantime. My first call was to preach the Gospel, and I felt I needed to get started on that right away. Needless to say, I quickly discovered that there would be many varied responses to my newborn ministry, even among my family and friends.

CHAPTER FOUR
BAPTIZED IN THE SPIRIT

Sixteen years in a dead church practicing an empty religion that they called "Christianity" had brought me to the brink of atheism, and I was a hair's breadth away from giving up on faith altogether. Now, however, for the first time in my life, I had witnessed true Christianity. I had experienced God's presence in my life, and had seen His power in action. All my life I thought I knew what I wanted to be—a scientist. Now I knew that God had a different purpose in mind—I was to be a preacher of the Gospel and a missionary to the Chinese people. From now on, my life would have a different focus and new priorities.

Once I had committed my life to Christ, it seemed perfectly natural to me that I should start sharing the Gospel right away. Having surrendered to God's call to preach, a sense of urgency burned in my heart. I felt like the Apostle Paul, who said, "I am compelled to preach. Woe to me if I do not preach the gospel!" (1 Cor. 9:16b NIV). Besides, having already resisted the Lord's call for three months, I felt I needed to make up for lost time. I began at school the very next day.

Before the first class period of band began, where I played the clarinet, I approached the director and asked, "Could I have a few minutes to speak to the rest of the students?"

"I'm sorry," he replied, "but we don't have time. We have to start practicing right away to get ready for Friday night's football game."

"But this is a matter of life and death," I insisted.

The band director gave me a look of disbelief, as if he thought I was exaggerating or being overly dramatic. Nevertheless, he relented. "Okay, I can give you five minutes."

I'm sure many of my fellow band members were surprised when I stood before them and began talking. After all, I was the same guy who, though thoroughly prepared, once got so nervous during an oral presentation in class, that I actually started crying in front of my classmates. Now I was standing before them and telling them about God, with no trace of nervousness or fear.

"I have been in the church all my life," I told them. "But it was only yesterday that I truly found the Lord and gave my life to Him to preach the Gospel. What I need to tell you is this—believe in Christ. Trust Him as your Savior and Lord, and you will have eternal life; otherwise, you will perish. The Bible says, 'For God so loved the world that He gave His only begotten Son, that whosoever believeth in Him should not perish, but have everlasting life' (John 3:16). The choice is yours. It really is a matter of life and death."

The band director said nothing, but the look on his face suggested that he may have regretted giving me the floor. Reaction from the band members was mixed. Some laughed at me and said, "Why are you preaching here in school? Keep your preaching in church, where it belongs." Others were more supportive. "This is great! We need more preachers of the Gospel. I hope you succeed in your vision."

So immediately, I encountered opposition as well as acceptance of the Gospel. Throughout the rest of that day, I continued to share the Gospel with students in other classes as I had the opportunity. I also joined the Christian student fellowship at school. In those days, no one ever told us that we could not pray or read the Bible in school. It was the year 1961, two years before the United States Supreme Court would outlaw praying in school and declare it unconstitutional. When I was in school, spiritual activities, such as praying, were perfectly normal for Christians. The only small opposition I received came from some individual students who did not believe in the Lord.

School was not the only place where I encountered opposition; I faced it at home as well. You would've thought that my father, as the son of a Pentecostal preacher, would have been happy about my decision to follow Christ and become involved in a Pentecostal church. He was not. He had no problem with my becoming a Christian, or even with going to church; he just did not want me going to that church. When I told my father that I'd given my life to the Lord, and decided to be a preacher, he said, "You can go to any church you want; you can go every day of the week, but do not go to that Pentecostal church."

"Why not?" I protested. "That is where I found the Lord. I've given my life to Jesus. It's a wonderful church. They are great people." I didn't understand at the time that he opposed my decision because he had been backslidden and not following the Lord. But there was no way I would keep going to the Methodist church, which had almost destroyed my faith in God, where they did not preach the Bible or Jesus Christ, but instead taught us that the Bible was full of fairy tales…and I told my father so. "I'm not going back to the Methodist church. I'm going to the Assembly of God church in El Monte."

As a new believer and preacher, I knew I needed all the training, Bible knowledge, and spiritual teaching I could get. And I committed myself to attend every service that I possibly could at the Assembly of God church in El Monte, where I had found the Lord.

My father became so angry that he threatened an ultimatum. "If you continue to go to that church, I will no longer consider you my son. You will not live in my house anymore."

This confrontation occurred literally as I was on my way out the door to go to church with Ron and his family (who usually gave me a ride to church because I had no car). I had not expected such a harsh reaction from my father, but what could I do? I did not want to lose my relationship with my father, but I also knew that I could not and would not abandon my newfound faith and the new direction and purpose in my life just to please him. During the hour-long ride to church, I pondered what to do.

After the service, I confided in Pastor McKay and told him what had happened. He sympathized with my plight and said, "I'm sure your father will get over this sooner or later, but until he does, you can stay with me."

As soon as I returned home, I started gathering my clothes and other personal belongings together. My father then walked into my room and saw me packing. "What are you doing?" he asked.

"I'm leaving," I replied. "You told me that I was no longer your son and could not live here any longer. Pastor McKay said that he would take me in."

My father seemed surprised that I had taken his words so seriously and that I was actually leaving. "Wait until tomorrow," he urged. "There's no rush to leave today. You can leave tomorrow." When tomorrow came around, he said again, "Don't go yet. Wait until tomorrow." This went on for several weeks. Meanwhile, I continued to go to the church in El Monte, until my father finally dropped the whole issue of my leaving home. I understand now that he probably never intended for me to take him literally. When he threatened to kick me out of the house for going to a Pentecostal church, he most likely was speaking out of anger at the moment, and then reconsidered his words later and realized he did not mean them. I think that in the beginning he thought this experience would be just a "religious fad" that I would tire of in a few weeks or months. At any rate, he eventually accepted my decision, even if he didn't like it.

Thankfully, I did not have to leave home at that time. After all, I was only 16 years old, had no money, and no practical means of providing for myself. But I would have left if my father had insisted I do so. The Lord had transformed my life so thoroughly, and it meant so much for me to serve Him, that I was willing to pay any price, even if it meant losing my home and becoming estranged from my father. I have always been thankful to God that it never had to come to that.

My mother's reaction to the news was different. When I told her that I had found the Lord, that He had called me into full-time ministry, and that I would probably go to Bible College after graduation from high school and then be a missionary overseas, she started to cry. This also was a response I had not anticipated. She seemed to be quite upset.

"What's wrong, Mother?" I asked. "Why are you crying?"

"For two reasons," she replied. "First, we have always been poor, and your father and I have never been able to properly provide for you. And many times you have expressed your desire to be a scientist, and because you are such an excellent student, I have always believed that you would succeed in that desire. I had hoped that you would go to the university, graduate with honors, get a good job in a scientific field, make a lot of money, and help support the family. But now you say you want to be a preacher. All the preachers I know have always been quite poor, including your grandfather. So you will probably never be able to help us out financially. We will probably be poor all our lives."

I had not given any thought to the effect my decision would have on the rest of my family. I started to respond, but my mother held up her hand. "But the real reason I am crying," she continued, "is because when I was young the Lord called me into ministry. I was even planning to go to Bible college to prepare myself. Instead, I married your father and gave birth to you. It is evident to me that the Lord's call on my life has come to you. These are tears of joy more than tears of sadness."

Immediately after turning to the Lord, I became extremely hungry for the baptism of the Holy Spirit. Once I had seen the power of God in action, witnessed people getting healed, and heard people speaking in tongues and prophesying, I knew I wanted that same Spirit-baptism for myself. Now that I had been born again through the blood of Christ, I loved Him with all my heart and wanted to be as close to Him as possible.

Pentecostals in those days believed you could be baptized in the Holy Spirit only after you had wholeheartedly sought the Lord, poured out your heart to Him, and committed yourself to living a holy life. They taught that God could not use an unholy vessel, so anyone seeking the baptism of the Holy Spirit had to be serious enough about it to confess and repent of all known sin.

I was so hungry for the Holy Spirit that I attended every meeting at the church that I possibly could. This included not only the Sunday morning service, but also the Sunday evening service, and the weekly Bible study service, which was usually held on a Thursday or a Friday. While the Sunday morning service was usually geared more toward worship and teaching for those who already knew the Lord, the Sunday evening service tended to be more evangelistic and revival-focused, aimed at people who were not yet believers.

One typical component of the Sunday evening service was prayer for the baptism of the Holy Spirit. After the conclusion of the main part of the service, an invitation went out for all those who had not yet received Spirit-baptism to come forward. The Spirit-filled believers in the room would then gather around them in a circle, that they called the "ring of fire," where they all began to pray loudly, shout, and speak in tongues. Quite often, this continued all night long, until every seeker, who had come forward, had received the baptism of the Spirit and was speaking in tongues. The whole affair was very loud, boisterous, and energetic.

I was immediately so hungry, so desperate for the Spirit on the same Sunday when I gave my heart to the Lord, that I went forward to receive prayer for the baptism of the Holy Spirit after the evening service on the same day. The "ring of fire" surrounded me and everyone began praying. Mixed in with the prayers were words of encouragement, such as, "Hold on, Brother," or "Just give up, Brother," or "Just give in to the Holy Spirit." At times, I did not know whether to hold on or to give up. "Lift your hands," they told me, so I did.

But for some reason, nothing happened.

The night wore on, and by five o'clock in the morning, we were still praying, and I still had not received the baptism of the Spirit. The prayer meeting eventually came to an end, because everybody had to leave to get ready to go to work. "But we'll be back next week," they promised, "and we'll keep on praying for you until you are baptized in the Holy Spirit."

I was so desperate for the baptism of the Holy Spirit that I actually became a little upset with the Lord for not giving me this gift right away. I could not understand it, because I had been so intense in my desire. A few days later, another event transpired that, while wonderful in one sense, added insult to injury in another.

As I mentioned before, during the first week after I was saved, I had witnessed for Christ in every one of my classes at school, beginning with the band members. Then that Friday, the band traveled with the football team to play at an away game. While riding on the bus, I witnessed to a guy sitting next to me, who was one of the saxophone players. I have long since forgotten his name, but I remember that he seemed to be open to my message even though he did not go to church and did not know the Lord.

"You need to repent of your sins," I told him. "You need to get saved, to accept Jesus Christ as your Savior and Lord. If you don't get saved, you will go to hell. But if you place your trust in Jesus and get saved, God will give you a wonderful life."

Although he appeared to listen, he did not commit his life to Christ while we were riding on the bus. Later during the game, the band performed on the field and then we sat down on the bleachers. Suddenly, my friend and I began to shake so violently that we could not stay in our seats; we kept falling off. It was very embarrassing, and everyone around us stared at us with strange looks and asked, "What's the matter with you guys? Are you having an epileptic attack?"

I said to my friend, "I think the Lord is dealing with you. You need to repent." Feeling uncomfortable with everyone watching us, we soon got up and went to the restroom, where we fell onto the floor and immediately began to call on the name of the Lord.

"Lord, forgive me!" my friend cried out. "Please save me!"

Within a minute, we both stopped shaking, and he began to laugh. He was so happy as he exclaimed, "I'm saved! Jesus has come into my heart!"

We then went back to our seats, and I immediately told several people, "My friend just got saved." Of course, they thought we were crazy. This was my first convert, only five days after giving my life to the Lord, and on that next Sunday, I took my friend to church with me. Although it was a regular service, at the end of the meeting, they decided to pray for people to receive the Holy Spirit. Both my friend and I went forward. Once again, I prayed fervently for the baptism of the Spirit, and others prayed for me as well. And once again, nothing happened. My friend, on the other hand, was baptized in the Spirit almost immediately. He had barely begun to pray when he suddenly broke out into a beautiful flow of tongues. Others told me later that they heard him speak in six different recognizable languages. My friend was extremely happy to have received the Holy Spirit and to speak in tongues, and I was also genuinely happy for him. At the same time, however, I was frustrated with God. "It's not fair," I told the Lord. "I came first! You should have given this to me first. Why does he get the baptism of the Holy Spirit, when I still don't have it?"

But what could I do? God is God, and His ways are beyond man's searching. Although I did not understand it, I had to trust that God had His reasons. It took me a long time, but eventually I learned that things that come easily also may be easily neglected…and I soon saw this truth borne out in the life of my friend. A few months after he was saved, he began attending parties, where there was dancing, drinking, and smoking (sometimes marijuana). One day I confronted him in love. "You shouldn't go to those parties," I told him. "They're not good for you."

In those days, Pentecostals did not ever go to movies, did not drink or smoke, and certainly did not go to parties where there was dancing and other kinds of worldly entertainment. Furthermore, many of these parties took place at the same time as the weekly prayer meetings or Bible studies were held at the church, so he was missing out on many services and training opportunities that he needed in order to grow as a new believer.

"I don't go there to dance or to do any of those other things," he protested. "I go because they invite me to play the saxophone. It's a way to build my musical career, and I can use those nightclubs and bars as a stepping-stone to bigger opportunities. I think I have a real shot at becoming a popular and successful saxophone player."

"God will open doors for you," I said, "if you trust Him and give Him time to do it in His way. You should not go to those kinds of places, or follow the ways of the world."

Unfortunately, he did not listen to me. He continued to go to parties, and within a few months fell away from following the Lord and stopped going to church altogether. I have never heard anything more from him. I do not know where he is today or where he stands with the Lord. It is truly sad, but illustrates the very real danger that worldly influences pose for Christian believers who are not careful and diligent about faithfully following the Lord and learning to rely on the strength and guidance of the Holy Spirit.

Unlike my friend who received the Holy Spirit so quickly, my quest for the baptism of the Spirit went on for months. The more I sought the Spirit's baptism, the hungrier and more desperate I became. In addition, my friend's apparent defection from the faith made me even more determined to receive the baptism of the Holy Spirit. I did not want to make the same decisions he had made.

At this point I need to make something very clear. The key to spiritual power, as I preach and teach everywhere I go, is not to seek the gifts of the Holy Spirit or even the gift of speaking in tongues, but to seek the baptism of the Holy Spirit. We seek the Holy Spirit Himself. Speaking in tongues is merely the initial and outward sign of the baptism of the Holy Spirit. To seek the baptism of the Holy Spirit is to seek the fullness of the presence of the Lord Himself.

For six months I had been seeking and praying for the baptism of the Holy Spirit, and many other people in the church had been praying for me as well. I was almost at my wits' end as to why God still denied me this gift despite my sincere desire. Then during Easter vacation of 1962, my parents bought a Greyhound bus ticket for me, and I went to El Centro to spend the holiday with my grandparents. At that time, both my grandparents worked for the Veterans Administration, so during the day I was alone in the house.

One day while my grandparents were at work, I got down on my knees to pray, and gave the Lord an ultimatum. "Lord," I begged, "this is the last time I am going to ask. For six full months I have been praying for the baptism of the Holy Spirit, yet You have not given it to me. I am desperate for the Spirit! Please, Lord, You have to fill me!"

Later during the morning, as I rummaged through my grandparents' large collection of record albums, I came across a recording of Handel's Messiah performed by the Mormon Tabernacle Choir. Although I did not put any stock in the Mormon faith, I felt that Handel's wonderful oratorio certainly had to be anointed by God's Spirit. God's Word, combined with Handel's glorious music, surely had to provide the makings for a wonderful worship experience. So I put the record on and began to worship the Lord. As the music progressed, and particularly during the great "Hallelujah Chorus," I totally forgot myself and began to bask in the Lord's presence.

As I knelt listening to the music, praying, and worshiping the Lord, all of a sudden I began to speak in what we call "stammering lips," a series of unusual sounds. I knew I wasn't speaking in tongues, but I also knew that it was something from outside myself, something that God was sending.

I was overjoyed. "Lord," I said, "I am so glad that I have finally met the Holy Spirit, but this is not enough. I want to speak in other tongues, like they did in Acts 2:4."

Within half an hour, I began to speak in tongues. A strange and beautiful language poured from my mouth, effortlessly, fluent and flowing. This was about 10 o'clock in the morning, and it continued throughout the day. I didn't want to stop, because I was afraid that if I did, it would go away. Some of the older Pentecostals in the church had told me that they had received the Holy Spirit many years before in a revival meeting, but had not spoken in tongues since then. This gave me the impression that the gift of tongues, once given, could depart very easily. The pastor reinforced this idea in my mind, by describing the Holy Spirit as being like a dove. Just as a dove can land on you, and then fly away, so also can the Holy Spirit. At least, that was the way I interpreted it in my youthful immaturity. For this reason, I feared that once I stopped speaking in tongues, the Holy Spirit would leave me. I had sought and prayed for this gift for so long, I did not want to lose it now that I had it. As I learned later, my fear was based on a misunderstanding of the Holy Spirit, and how He works.

At about 5:30 that afternoon, my grandmother came home. "How are you, Dennis?" she greeted me. When I responded in tongues, she was shocked, and asked me several more questions, but still could not understand what I was saying. A short time later, my grandfather also arrived from work, and the same thing happened. He asked me questions, and I also answered him in tongues.

My grandparents became quite upset, and even began to cry. "Oh, we should never have let you go to the Pentecostal church! We should have insisted that you stay in the Methodist church. We knew that you would have this problem!"

They actually thought I was mentally ill, that somehow my association with those Pentecostals had driven me crazy. "What are we going to do with him?" they wondered. Although the situation was a little tense for a while, they did eventually come to a better understanding of what I was doing.

I continued to speak in tongues until late that night. Finally, around 11:30, I was too tired to stay awake any longer, so I said, "Lord, I need to go to sleep, but please don't let the Holy Spirit fly away and leave me." And when I woke up at around six o'clock the following morning, the first thing on my mind was to find out if the Holy Spirit was still with me. And when I opened my mouth, I immediately began to speak in tongues. What a relief! I knew then that the Holy Spirit was indeed with me, and that He would never leave me. I have been praying in tongues daily ever since.

CHAPTER FIVE
PREACHER IN TRAINING

One of the first lessons I learned after giving my life to the Lord, is that old habits die hard and old mind-sets make for easy temptation. As I previously mentioned, before I surrendered to God's call to preach the Gospel, I had wanted to be a scientist. I enjoyed science classes in school, and particularly liked conducting scientific experiments, even at home. My parents also encouraged me in this field by spending a fair amount of their scarce and hard-earned money to buy chemicals and scientific equipment for my home laboratory.

In the meantime, when I answered God's call to preach the Gospel, I knew I was making a full-time commitment, which meant I would have to give up my time-consuming involvement in experiments, as well as my original dream of being a scientist. In the initial fervor of excitement surrounding my conversion and call to ministry, I found it easy to make that sacrifice...or so I thought. I soon discovered, however, that my old desire would not give up without a fight.

Several months went by after my conversion and call, and I was continuing to attend every church service and meeting that I possibly could, which meant not only the Sunday morning and evening services, but also the Friday night prayer meeting/Bible study. I was so caught up in the Lord that I did not give a second thought to science. After a while, however, I began to miss that old life and found myself thinking, I sure do love science. It's been a long time since I did an experiment. I really miss it.

So, one Friday afternoon, I surrendered to the urge. I knew I had enough time to get an experiment in before leaving for church with my friend Ron and his family. For the moment, I ignored what the Lord had already told me very clearly—that I was to give up the science experiments and apply myself to Bible study and preaching, because I was no longer training to be a scientist, but a preacher.

The experiment I chose that Friday afternoon involved the use of nitric acid, a very dangerous and corrosive acid, particularly in undiluted form. In the course of the experiment, a volatile reaction of chemicals caused the test tube to explode—not a big explosion, but powerful enough to splash nitric acid into one of my eyes. Immediately, my eye was engulfed in excruciating, burning pain, and I could no longer see through it. I rushed to a mirror and examined myself. The affected eye was milky, clouded over with what looked like cataracts. A bolt of fear shot through my mind. Would I be blind in that eye for the rest of my life? "Lord, please help me!" I cried. "I'm sorry, Lord. I know You told me to give this up. I repent! Please forgive me. Please heal me. I promise I will never touch the stuff again." That is when I began to realize that there were some things that would always be a temptation for me; things that were not bad in and of themselves, but wrong for me because they would divert my attention from what God had called me to do.

The accident happened only about ten minutes before I was due to leave for church, so I had just enough time to grab a pair of dark glasses to hide my injury. Although I am sure that Ron and the other members of his family were curious about the sunglasses; mercifully, no one asked me about them. During the hour-long drive to church, and throughout the service, my eye was still quite painful, and silently, I kept reiterating my promise to the Lord - that if He healed me, I would never touch those chemicals or any scientific paraphernalia again.

That evening, the church service went quite well. The Holy Spirit was moving in power, and I got so caught up in prayer and the spirit of worship, that I almost forgot about my eye. By the time the service was over, I realized that my eye did not hurt anymore, and even more so, I could see with it again. I walked into the restroom and looked in the mirror. My eye was completely normal—no cloudiness, no scarring, no pain. God had healed me completely!

Upon arriving home that night, I immediately gathered all my chemicals and other laboratory equipment and threw it away. My father caught me in the middle of the act.

"What are you doing?" he challenged. "We spent all this money to buy this scientific equipment for you because you said you wanted to be a scientist. You know that we don't have a whole lot of money, and yet here you are, throwing it all away. Why?"

"The Lord has called me to be a preacher," I reminded him. Then I told him about the accident to my eye, and how God had healed me. He looked at me like he thought I was crazy. At that time, my father, despite his Pentecostal background, apparently was not ready or able to understand that kind of divine power at work so specifically in a person's life. I know that he was unhappy with my decision, but there was very little he could do. I had no desire to hurt or disappoint my father, but that was the price I had to pay in order to be obedient to the Lord. Thankfully, my father came around to the idea later, just as he had when he threatened to throw me out of the house for going to a Pentecostal church.

Another challenge I faced after surrendering to God's call to the ministry, was finding opportunities to preach. I wanted to preach right away, but I couldn't very well go to the pastor and ask, "Will you let me preach next Sunday?" After all, I had just been saved, and I had no preaching experience. Furthermore, I didn't even know if I could preach. Yet I would never know until I tried. Once or twice I was given the opportunity to share in the youth meeting, and I expected that somehow I would eventually go to Bible College…but that was still a couple of years away. What was I to do in the meantime? I wanted to start fulfilling God's call as soon as I could. I really wanted to preach…right away.

In those days, we did a lot of door-to-door witnessing. That was easier then than it is today, partly because of restrictions in some areas, and partly because people today, thanks to groups like the Jehovah's Witnesses and the Mormons, tend to be more cautious of strangers at their door and less open to conversation. Back then, however, we witnessed to many people on the street and door to door, and handed out gospel tracts by the hundreds. We would talk to anyone who would listen and invite them to church. In addition to the door-to-door evangelism, we also held street meetings, where we would stand on street corners and preach to people passing by. I was totally involved in all these activities, because I was so hungry for opportunities to preach.

Then one day I heard about a "skid row" mission in Los Angeles—an evangelistic outreach program run by a local church organization that specifically targeted the "down-and-out" people of the city—pimps, prostitutes, and others who lived in the red-light district, as well as alcoholics, drug addicts, the homeless, and the unemployed.

The mission always offered a daily meal. It was not a great meal—but when you are unemployed or homeless and have no money or a place to sleep, at least it was food and provided nourishment. There was only one condition to get the meal—the people had to first come to a meeting, which began at six o'clock sharp. Anyone who wanted to eat the meal served after the meeting had to be in the building before the doors closed at six o'clock. Latecomers missed out. Despite this restriction, the building was usually full. There were a lot of hungry people on the streets of L.A.

The service was usually very simple. They would sing a few songs, and then someone would get up to preach. It was not an easy task to get preachers to come to a place like that. Many church people, including preachers, felt uncomfortable around the types of people who came to the mission—they were dirty, drunk, destitute, high, hung over, and strung out. In addition, the mission had little or no money to pay a preacher. The down-and-outs who came certainly did not have any, and the people in charge usually had barely enough money to pay for the meals and the costs of running the mission.

Even so, when I heard about the place, I contacted the people in charge and asked, "Can I come and preach?"

"Sure," they replied. "Anybody can preach here. If you are saved, you can preach."

During the next couple years, I visited that mission often and preached to the people there. In one of his books, Dr. Paul Yonggi Cho talks about what he calls the "fourth dimension." He recalls the times early in his ministry when he would preach in a church of several hundred people, yet imagine that he was preaching to a thousand. Then, when he was preaching to a thousand, he would imagine that he was preaching to ten thousand. He understood the importance of thinking big and dreaming big. That mind-set helped him build the largest church in the world. Likewise, in my youthful enthusiasm and inexperience, I would think while preaching in that Los Angeles mission, "I'm Billy Graham number two," or, "I'm Billy Sunday number two." I was preaching like a house on fire, "You guys have got to repent, because Jesus is coming soon!"

The fact is, however, half the people in the meeting were asleep, while the other half showed little interest in what I had to say. Most of them were alcoholics or drug addicts, after all. But it was a chance for me to preach and to learn how to be comfortable in front of people. At the end of every service I gave an altar call, and usually, almost without exception, everybody there would raise their hand indicating they wanted prayer or wanted to be saved. At first, that kind of response really excited me, but then I learned that in this kind of setting, that reaction was commonplace and usually did not mean much. Many would come forward to cry, and even to pray, but they were people with deep-seated addictions and other physical, mental, or emotional dysfunctions; and very few people actually were set free from their problems. Of course, the power of the Holy Spirit can deliver even the worst addict instantaneously, but it rarely happens that way. Normally, helping people to kick the habits of alcohol or drugs is very difficult, because those addictions are so strong.

This particular mission was not Pentecostal or charismatic, and we were not there long enough to teach them about the baptism of the Holy Spirit; but we did pray with them, and we shared the love of Christ with themand told them of His power to save them and change their lives. We saw a few victories, a few people whose lives were transformed miraculously by the power of Christ. But the most important result that came out of my two-year association with this skid row mission in L.A., was that I learned to preach.

Then, in the spring of 1963, I graduated from Los Altos High School in L.A. County, and in September of that year, I enrolled as a full-time student at Southern California Bible College (now Vanguard University), an Assemblies of God-affiliated school in Costa Mesa. This time was a significant turning point in my life because, from that point on, I was on my own. After leaving for Bible college, I never returned home, except for occasional brief visits.

From the time I became a Christian until the day I left home, I did my best to witness to my parents and to my brothers and sisters. However, they would not listen, and not one of them would follow me to the Assembly of God church. It is always the most difficult to witness to your own family, because they know you with all your faults. But I refused to give up. Never a day passed that I did not pray for them, calling out the names of each and every one before the Lord. Several years later, while I was in the Army and posted to Vietnam, a fervent Baptist neighbor built a relationship with my family and drew them into the Baptist church. There, after a short time, they all gave their lives to the Lord and were born again. My prayers were answered. I have always been thankful for that faithful Baptist believer who practiced evangelism personally, and helped the members of my family find eternal life in Christ.

Enrolling in Bible college was a personal act of faith for me because I had no money to pay my tuition, and neither did my parents. Nevertheless, the Lord provided in wonderful, sometimes miraculous ways. After I arrived on campus, I found a part-time job as a janitor for the school in a work-study arrangement. My wage was one dollar an hour. That doesn't sound like much these days, and perhaps it wasn't even then, but it was enough because God provided, and His provision is always sufficient. My total school fees amounted to $100 a month. This meant that the most I could make every month was $100. But I was committed to first paying a tithe or ten percent, which then left me with $90. Still, it was amazing how the Lord provided during my one year at the school. I never missed a single monthly payment. Somehow, no matter what my expenses were for any given month, or what kind of shortfall I had, money always came my way in time to meet the due date of my payment.

I know this gift was of God, because I was not well known and was not even a bona fide preacher yet; but for some reason, people would give me money. On one particular day, I was walking to the registrar's office where I intended to pay part of my school fees. I don't remember how much money I had, but I know it was not enough. Meanwhile, along the way, someone walked up and handed me an envelope. I stuck it in my pocket and kept walking. When I arrived at the registrar's office, I opened the envelope and discovered that it was filled with cash. Combined with the money I already had, the cash in the envelope brought the total to exactly $100; not a penny more, nor a penny less. This kind of thing happened throughout the entire year.

In addition to providing finances, although meager, my janitorial job also rendered a rich life experience. Specifically, it was my job to clean the toilets in all the dormitories, including the men's and the women's dormitories, where the residents on each floor shared a common restroom. Whenever I entered the women's dormitories, I had to call out a warning, "Man in the dorm," so that female residents would vacate the restrooms. And in all the dormitories, clogged toilets were commonplace. You would not believe some of the things that college students try to flush down the toilets! I learned very quickly that the only way to get that stuff out was to reach in and physically pull it out with my hand. I could not use any kind of instrument; it was literally "manual" labor.

As distasteful and disgusting as this work was, it taught me the value of doing a thorough job, even on the dirtiest and most unpleasant of tasks. One of the things I did when I came to Hong Kong was teach the people how to clean a toilet—how to get "down and dirty" and really clean it. I believe it is no exaggeration to say that such a job can build your character. It certainly did mine. It taught me that no job is too menial, and a job done well, even a menial one, can bring glory to God.

Another part of my job was driving a dump truck in order to transport trash from the school to the dump. It was an old truck, somewhat battered and worn, and was not in the best operating condition. For instance, the clutch did not work very well. In fact, shifting from first gear to second gear and from second to third was often a challenge. That was bad enough, but to make things worse, the "dump" function of the truck did not even work. This meant that I had to physically climb into the bed of the truck, in the midst of all the garbage, and push it out by hand.

Working as a janitor was a hot, dirty, and often disgusting job, but I didn't care. I was called to preach the Gospel, and I was willing to pay any price to get my education. It did not matter that the job was demeaning by using my hands to clean out toilets and as a shovel to empty garbage at the dump. It was a necessary job, and it supported me for an entire year. Today, I would not trade this experience for anything in the world.

In addition to character, the job helped me learn discipline. Many students there, both male and female, did not have to work at all, either because they were children of pastors, or because their parents had money. Most of them were completely undisciplined and didn't apply themselves to their studies. As a result, they earned mediocre grades, and some of them even flunked out. There was a saying around campus that Southern California Bible College was actually Southern California "Bridal" College, because it seemed that many of the students simply came to find a spouse rather than to earn a degree. I discovered that even though the school was a "Christian" college, and most of the students came from a Christian home, many of them were not serving the Lord, and a fair number probably were not even saved.

As it turned out, I attended that school for only one year...for a couple of reasons. At the time I enrolled, the college was working hard to earn its accreditation...too hard in my opinion. In 1962, the year before I arrived, the college had invited the accreditation association to come and investigate the school. The college had completed all the preliminary requirements, submitted the necessary paperwork, and met all the basic qualifications, but the accreditation association still had to make a personal visit and conduct a final evaluation. While Southern California Bible College was affiliated with the Assemblies of God, the accreditation association either was secular or, if Christian, was of a non-Pentecostal nature. One day the evaluators were observing a theology class when the professor suffered an apparent heart attack right there in class. Today, the immediate response would be to call 911, but on that day back in 1962, the students in that class did what all good Pentecostals would've done—they prayed. The room was filled with students lifting their hands and praying loudly in tongues. In a matter of minutes, the Lord healed the stricken professor. He stood up and continued teaching as if nothing had happened. This incident did not sit well with the accreditation evaluators, who had never seen anything this "crazy." As a result of just this one incident, the accreditation association rejected the school's accreditation application.

The next year, the year I enrolled, the school attempted to gain accreditation again, and they were determined not to let anything spoil their chances this time around. For this reason, they instructed the student body not to pray in class for any reason. If we needed to pray, we were to go to the chapel to do so.

Understandably, several students were shocked and upset about this decision. We could not even pray in class? How could that be? This was a Bible college, a school established originally to train missionaries! And now we were being told we could not pray in class, simply to ensure that the school received its accreditation. Well...no one got sick, no one had a heart attack, no one prayed in tongues in class...and the school received its accreditation. But it lost something even more important. From that time forward, the spiritual dynamic and figure of the school began to diminish, and that decline has continued until the present day. Essentially, the Holy Spirit left. Today,

Southern California Bible College is known as Vanguard University, has strayed far from its evangelical and Pentecostal roots, and is now more secular than Christian.

Spiritual compromise at the school was bad enough, but what really sealed my decision to leave was the experience of a fellow student named Robert Bailey. For some time, Robert had been attending a church in Long Beach called Bethany Chapel. Long Beach was quite a distance from Costa Mesa, where the college was located. On occasion, Bethany Chapel held what were called presbytery meetings, where leaders would prophesy over people and help them receive the baptism of the Holy Spirit. Robert attended several of these, and I remember him returning to school one day after attending one of these meetings. He looked like he had been to Heaven. Robert's face was like that of an angel; it almost glowed with the presence and the glory of God.

A group of us gathered around him, extremely curious at the change that had come over him. "What happened to you?"

"I cannot even begin to describe it," he replied, with awe and excitement in his voice. "You need to come and see for yourselves."

So we did. The next week I, along with 11 others, went with Robert to Bethany Chapel, traveling in two cars. At that time, David Schoch was the pastor. He was quite prophetic himself, but also invited many other speakers who were known in that day as "latter rain" prophets.

During these presbytery meetings, leaders would instruct the people who wanted to receive a prophecy from the Lord to pray and fast for three days, drinking only water. Then, at the next meeting, those people who had fasted would sit in the front, and the leaders, if they felt so led, would call each person forward individually. There was no rush. They took their time with each individual, prophesying to that person as they received a word from the Lord. Each prophecy was recorded, and afterward, the presbytery pastor reviewed each prophecy with the person who had received it to make sure the person agreed with everything and understood how to apply the prophecy in his or her life. The reason for the presbytery, with multiple leaders involved, was for safety's sake. If one person happened to "miss it" on a prophecy, someone else would be there to provide the correction.

The day we attended, we all sat on the front row, even though none of us were "ready"—none of us had fasted and prayed. Nevertheless, these prophets called up every one of the students except me, and prophesied over them. I was absolutely amazed at what I heard, because I personally knew these students, and the prophets correctly described in accurate detail the call of God on their lives, their strengths, their weaknesses, and even more. Some people were singers, while others had a teaching or preaching ministry. Whatever it was, everything came forward so very clearly. This impressed me so much that I immediately decided that this was the church I wanted to be part of. I had attended a few of the Assemblies of God churches in that area, but they were quite dead, in my opinion. In fact, some of them, in order to be accepted by other people, did not allow speaking in tongues in the public service. They insisted, "If you want to pray in tongues, you can go to the prayer room."

I wanted to be part of a church that openly welcomed the Holy Spirit. Bethany Chapel was such a church. What made it even more appealing was that the church offered its own Bible training program, including Bible and missionary training classes several times a week, although it was not a full-time Bible school and was not accredited. The lack of accreditation didn't bother me. It was much more important for me to study the Bible and worship in an environment where the Holy Spirit was welcome and was working in power.

Bethany Chapel and other churches that fully embraced the "latter rain" revival and restoration movement that began in the 1940s received tremendous opposition from the Assemblies of God, which thought the movement and its leaders were a cult. Some of the criticism was valid. There were some leaders of the movement who went off on tangents and got themselves into serious error, both biblically and doctrinally. Some were brought down by moral scandals, and a few even went to jail. These were a distinct minority, however. The vast majority of latter rain churches and leaders remained true to the Bible and to the work of the Holy Spirit. Bethany Chapel in Long Beach was one of them. It was such a lively church and with such an obvious presence of the Holy Spirit, that I knew it was the church for me.

So I left Costa Mesa and Southern California Bible College, and moved to Long Beach. By this time, fortunately, I had my own car. A couple of years previously, while still in high school, my father had given me a car, an old 1950's model that needed some work. He fiddled with it off and on, trying to get it to run for years, but it wasn't until after I graduated from high school that he succeeded. But even though I had a car, I probably had less than ten dollars to my name. Of course, gasoline was much cheaper than it is today, no more than 15 or 20 cents a gallon, so I was able to buy enough gasoline to get me to Long Beach. But that's about all I had. I had no job, no place to stay, and no money for rent, even if I could have found a place. Furthermore, I did not forewarn anybody at the church that I was coming. With nowhere else to go, I parked in the church parking lot and slept in the car. I wasn't really worried. I was too excited and too hungry for the Holy Spirit and for the Word of God to be worried. And I was still young and rather impulsive; it all seemed like a great adventure to me.

After a few days, the church secretary noticed that I was there. "Where are you sleeping?" she asked.

"In the church parking lot."

"Don't you have a place to stay?"

When she found out I didn't, she went into immediate action. The church staff talked with me and helped me find a place I could rent very cheap. Not long after, I found a job. It didn't pay much, no more than a dollar or so an hour, but I didn't care. It was a job. Besides, I wasn't interested in making money. I just wanted to get into the Bible. I wanted to be a part of this church because I saw God was there.

Eventually, I found a job working in the kitchen of California State University in Long Beach. In addition to the low pay, it would be a very hot job—working around steam, scalding dishwater, and big industrial-size ovens all day.

Interestingly, on my second day on the job, the head chef came up to me and said, "Young man, we are looking for someone to train to be a chef. Would you be interested in this position?"

"I don't know anything about food preparation," I replied.

"Don't worry," he said. "We'll train you. Are you interested?"

"Well," I said, "it's a lot better than washing pots and pans. Yeah, I'm interested."

So I began learning how to be a chef. I was part of a team who cooked meals for the entire university, which numbered 25,000 students, not counting faculty and administration. We prepared much of the food in huge pots in the kitchen, which we would stir with big paddles, while steam swirled around our heads. When making stew, we would put in 100 pounds of potatoes, 50 pounds of carrots, 50 pounds of beef, and whatever else, and then add two or three handfuls of salt. After stirring everything together, we would conduct a taste test to make sure the stew was seasoned enough. I was usually involved in preparing the main course, such as the meat and vegetables. There were other employees who prepared desserts and pastries and other food items. Learning to cook in such an environment was a valuable skill that served me well in the Army later, but it was not very practical in a family setting. My wife will now tell you that in the early years of our marriage, whenever I cooked for the two of us, I always ended up making far more than we could finish, because I had been trained to cook in large amounts. Eventually, I learned to adapt.

I had been in Long Beach for only a few weeks when I was hit by another driver who ran a red light and demolished my car. Fortunately, neither of us was injured. Although the accident was not my fault, the other driver had no insurance, and consequently never paid for the damages to my car. And because I did not have the money to buy another car, I came to the conclusion that God did not want me to have one. So I bought a bicycle, which turned out to be a good idea. It was a very nice 10-speed bicycle, and I rode it everywhere—to work, church, shopping, and anywhere else I needed or wanted to go. Sometimes I even rode all the way to Chinatown in Los Angeles, a distance of over 20 miles one way. Riding that bicycle was great exercise, both physically and spiritually. It strengthened my body, built up my endurance, and gave me plenty of time to pray and worship the Lord.

Earlier in the day, before the accident had occurred, I had been reading in the Book of Revelation—"Babylon has fallen, Babylon has fallen." Now I was standing next to a demolished car on a street lined with jewelry and electronics stores. There were expensive goods on display in the store windows all around me, and a thought entered my mind that I believe was put there by the Lord. All these things will be gone someday. Material things are not important. You are here because you want to serve the Lord. God wants you to really get into His Word, because you're called to preach the Gospel.

Losing my car would provide another lesson from God. All my life growing up, God had taught me to live simple. And I always have. Even today in Hong Kong, my wife, Kathy, and I rent our flat; the vehicle we drive belongs to the church; and we receive a very modest salary that would probably be considered below the poverty line by most people, especially by U.S. standards. But the Lord has always provided for every need, and He continues to do so. Early on, we learned the value of giving generously even when our own means were modest. And no matter how much we have given, we have never lacked anything we needed.

If you read older books about missionaries and missionary training, you will find one common thread that weaves through them all: "Expect to live a life of poverty." This is the exact opposite advice to the prosperity message so many are preaching today. To anyone who may be contemplating a call to missions work, let me say this: Don't come into this work expecting a cushy salary and an affluent lifestyle. God may bless you that way, and He may not...probably not. But there are many other riches that will come your way that are much more satisfying than material prosperity—rewards that carry eternal significance both for you and for the people you serve with the Gospel of Christ. One thing is certain—if you are really called of God to this work, you will make it. He will see to it.

CHAPTER SIX
HOLY SPIRIT POWER

From the very beginning, the baptism of the Holy Spirit has been the core teaching of my ministry. I make no apology for this decision, because I believe in honoring the Holy Spirit. Of course, I always preach the centrality of Christ and the need for every person to receive and acknowledge Jesus Christ as his or her personal Savior and Lord. Salvation in Christ is the message of the Gospel and the key prerequisite to receiving the baptism or power of the Holy Spirit, which enables us as Christians to put our faith into practical action.

I am passionate about the Holy Spirit, because ever since that day when I gave my life to the Lord at the age of 16, I have continually witnessed His power in my own life as well as in the lives of others. I first witnessed it in the Assembly of God church in El Monte, and continued to experience it after I went to Bethany Chapel. During my years there, I saw the Lord work in exciting and mighty ways over and over again.

I remember attending a healing crusade, conducted by a man named Leroy Jenkins, who is still preaching today with an amazing healing testimony of his own. A nominal believer, he had one day walked through a plate glass window, which almost cut off his arm and leaving only a few muscles and nerve endings intact. Emergency medical responders wanted to amputate his arm, but he would not allow it.

Subsequently, as they were on the way to the hospital, the ambulance passed by a healing crusade led by a man named A. Allen. On impulse, Leroy Jenkins insisted that they stop, so they carried him inside, where A. Allen prayed for him. In answer to that prayer, God completely healed Leroy Jenkins, and his arm was completely restored. He then responded to God's call to be a preacher and embarked on an amazing Spirit-filled healing ministry of his own.

I remember one of his meetings in Long Beach where the miracles were simply unbelievable. In one instance, after he had prayed for six people who were confined to wheelchairs, five of them immediately got up and began to walk. That same night, I was seated on the second row directly behind a young lady who was about 23 years old. I thought she was pregnant, because she had an enlarged belly and was wearing what appeared to be a maternity dress. At one point, Jenkins walked up to her and said, "The Lord gave me a word that you have severe, late-stage stomach cancer. It has completely filled your abdominal cavity. In fact, you saw your doctor at four o'clock this afternoon, and he told you that you probably have, at most, two weeks to live."

She began to cry and said, "How did you know that? It's all true; I have cancer and have been told I have only two weeks to live."

"But I have another word for you, Sister," Jenkins said. "God is going to heal you." Then he looked up and spoke to the crowd. "Don't close your eyes," he instructed. "You need to see this."

Of course, I wanted to see it, and being that I was closer to her than just about anyone else in the room, I had a great vantage point. Brother Jenkins did not lay hands on her or touch her physically in any way. He simply spoke some sort of command; I do not recall exactly what he said, but I do remember it was very short. What happened next was absolutely amazing. Even as I, and everyone else in the room, watched, her belly deflated—pssshhh—like a balloon that had been punctured. In a matter of moments, she went from being a very large woman to a very small woman. The guy sitting next to me, his eyes as round as saucers, said, "Did you see that?" We were standing right behind her; we could not help but see it! This was no trick; it was a healing like none I had ever seen before. Her cancer literally disappeared before my eyes.

This is the kind of Holy Spirit power I was a constant witness to in those days; so is it any wonder that I would make the baptism of the Holy Spirit such a central part of my own ministry? I'm not saying that miracles always occurred; they did not. Not everyone who received prayer for healing was healed. But it happened often enough to make it clear that the Holy Spirit was at work.

Oral Roberts, the great healing evangelist who came to Long Beach for a crusade on one occasion, shared a perspective that I have remembered through the years. Personally a very humble man, he acknowledged, "You may see a lot of miracles, but don't think for a moment that I am a great healing evangelist. I pray for hundreds of people every day, and only five percent of them are healed." That may have been true; but the way I look at it, if you pray for a thousand people every day and "only five percent of them are healed," you're still going to see a lot of people healed! The important action to take is to pray for healing and let the Holy Spirit do the rest, rather than assume there will be no healing and not pray at all.

One time at Bethany Chapel, Pastor David Schoch called out a woman specifically and said to her, "I have a word of knowledge for you." That's the way it was done in those days. The leader would call out a specific person, tell that person the word he or she had received from the Lord, and then ask the person if the word was true. "Is this so? I want to know for confirmation." It is different today. Today, the leader will say, "There is someone in this meeting with such-and-such a condition; please come forward or raise your hand." There is nothing wrong with sharing a word with someone this way, but I still remember with great affection the way they did it in the "old days."

On that particular day in Bethany Chapel, David Schoch said to the woman, "This is a word of knowledge from the Lord. I see that you have been to the doctor, and that you cannot have a baby. You have been married for a few years, but the doctors have told you not to get pregnant, because it could be dangerous. Your pelvic bone is out of position. If you try to have a baby, the baby may die."

"Yes, that's right!" the woman acknowledged, astonished.

"Sister," Pastor Schoch continued, "I have a creative word for you: God is going to heal you, and you are going to have a baby next year at this time. I want you to go back to your doctor and get a new report. Then come back next week and show us what the Lord has done for you."

She did. The next week she was back, her face aglow with joy. She mounted the platform and held up two separate x-rays. Pointing to one, she said, "This is the x-ray taken a few months ago. And this," pointing to the other, "is the one taken this week. The bones have actually changed their location; they have moved." She was right. The evidence was right there on the x-rays, clear enough for everyone in the room to see. "This is quite a big miracle, for the bones in my body to move," she continued. "The best part of all is that the doctor has said I can now have a baby." Sure enough, nine or ten months later, she gave birth. I remember the day she brought her newborn son to church and dedicated him to the Lord.

While we were learning a lot about integrity and the importance of solid doctrine, church life in those days was also filled with miraculous happenings. It was a time when miracles and spiritual gifts were very common and extremely powerful. Maybe that was good, and maybe it wasn't; that debate has been going on for years without resolution. I am convinced, however, that God was restoring these things to demonstrate anew the power of the Gospel. By the end of World War II, the spiritual condition of the whole world in general, and of America in particular, was at a low ebb. Even most of the Pentecostal churches were not following the Lord. Several well-known leaders and numerous churches of the day went off into error and departed from sound biblical doctrine and truth. The nation was ripe for revival, and before long, it came.

In 1948, God ushered in what came to be known as the "latter rain revival," which was characterized by the appearance of a number of prominent healing evangelists such as A. Allen, Kathryn Kuhlman, Oral Roberts, and others. This revival was a restoration movement that brought the focus of the church back onto the supremacy and sovereignty of Christ, and the living, active power of the Holy Spirit.

Bethany Chapel moved in this revival, and because I was a part of that church, I did too. Today, I recognize how truly blessed I am to have done so. Every success, every advance, every achievement that has been gained in my ministry in Hong Kong and in mainland China is a legacy, an outgrowth of the latter rain restoration movement of the Holy Spirit.

So, moving to Long Beach proved to be a good choice for me. Bethany Chapel had a great Bible training program, and I soaked up everything I could. Although it was not an accredited program where you could earn a degree, I learned more there than I ever would have had I stayed at the Bible college. My job as a cook in the university kitchen was also a blessing, because my work schedule allowed me plenty of time to pray, attend Bible classes, and dig deep into the Word of God.

I was also able to spend a significant amount of time with Pastor David Schoch in a mentoring relationship. At one point, I asked him if I could accompany him on one of his many ministering trips, even if it was just to carry his briefcase. That's how hungry I was. For almost five years, as my schedule allowed, I then accompanied him from city to city and meeting to meeting and witnessed his prophetic gift in action. We would go to a place where we had never been before, where he did not know anyone, yet would stand up and share detailed information about their lives—what was currently happening to them, and what was going to happen.

Even before I went to Vietnam in the mid-1960s, he prophesied very clearly that America would lose that war, which is exactly what happened. He prophesied that the U.S. would go into Cambodia, and that also happened. In 1962, before I knew him, he prophesied that President Kennedy would be assassinated. Indeed, President Kennedy was murdered in November 1963, a crime that the people in David Schoch's church knew about a year in advance. He prophesied many world events, and he was very accurate in his words of knowledge. A few years ago, he passed on to glory, and to this day, I feel blessed and honored to have been associated with him.

One time Pastor Schoch challenged us all to a three-day fast in which we would eat nothing at all and drink only water. During the fast, there would be prayer, worship, and Bible study meetings at the church both morning and evening. I had never really fasted before, but I challenged myself to not only fast for three days, but for five days. Needless to say, this did not go over well with my boss at the kitchen. Although he was a Christian, a Baptist in fact, he did not understand or believe in fasting, and was worried about me.

"How can you dare go without food?" he asked me. "You're going to die! I don't want you to die while working in my kitchen!"

"Don't worry," I assured him. "I'm fine."

Still, he wasn't satisfied. "I'd like to take your pastor and string him up for making you fast," he complained.

"But he is not making me fast," I argued. "I am doing this because I want to. My pastor has called the church to a three-day fast, but I'm the one who has chosen to fast for five days."

During the fast, I still had to taste the food while preparing it, which was one of my responsibilities as a cook. But I always immediately washed my mouth out after conducting the test. For five days, I ate nothing at all. Yet I never got hungry, and I never grew weak. I even discovered that I really enjoyed fasting. Best of all, I learned to pray with more power and drew closer to the Lord.

My job as a chef was a great fit for my lifestyle of spiritual growth and ministry at Bethany Chapel. I worked the morning shift, which meant that following the afternoon meal, I was finished working for the day. Every morning I reported to work at four o'clock –five o'clock at the latest—to prepare breakfast, stayed through to prepare the noon meal, and then left around three o'clock in the afternoon after washing the pots, pans, and other dishware. This left me with enough time to go home, clean up, and make it to the evening Bible training classes at the church. My life was simple. I was single, lived in a rented room of a house, and rode my bicycle to and from work and other places, except church, which was too far away. It was a wonderful time. I was up every morning, riding my bike to work, praying in the Holy Spirit along the way, working my job, riding home, cleaning up, reading my Bible, and then heading off to church for training.

The only drawback was that I had no job in the summer, because the university was not in session, except for a few classes. One summer I decided not to search for another job but chose instead to spend more time with the Lord and read my Bible. That meant I had to live as cheaply as possible. When I went to the market, I would buy inexpensive food items like spaghetti, macaroni, potatoes, and beans. For three months, I did not eat any meat or vegetables. Unfortunately, my body rebelled against this mistreatment, and I developed a severe red skin condition. I itched all the time and could not find relief. Somehow my mother found out about my illness and took me to a doctor, who prescribed a special kind of ointment. Fortunately, it was very powerful and helped stop the itching. However, it was very expensive—$20 for a tiny tube (and that's 1960s dollars!); therefore, we could not afford more than one or two tubes. I was broke, and at that time my family was not much better off. I then decided that it was time to pray and ask the Lord to heal me.

I prayed for healing faithfully for several months, but to no avail. This really amazed and confused me, because every other time I prayed, God always came through. Other people also prayed. Pastor Schoch even prayed for me. We continued to see other people healed, yet I still suffered sleepless nights as the days and weeks went by.

One night, fighting discouragement and disappointment, I got up and walked through the house praying. I had many questions. What is wrong? Does God hear my prayers? Why doesn't He heal me? The more I prayed and the more I thought about the situation, however, the more I began to see the whole experience in a different light. Sure, I am in pain, I thought, but there are a lot of people who are in worse condition than I am. And anyhow, I'm going to Heaven someday, and then I will not be in this body any longer. I will be whole, healed, and busy worshiping the Lord. Even if I have this skin condition all my life, it will only be for so many years, and then I'll be in eternity with the Lord, and all this will be behind me.

I remember praying, "Lord, I believe You are going to heal me, but even if You choose not to heal me, that's okay; I will still worship You. I will still follow You. I will still preach the Gospel. Even if You don't let me into Heaven, I will still worship You, and I will still follow You, because You are God, and You are worthy of all my praise. If I end up in hell, I will start a big prayer meeting in hell, and we all will worship You down there."

That's how strongly I felt about worshiping and serving the Lord. Somehow, reaching that mind-set gave me peace, and I was able to go to sleep at about five o'clock in the morning. When I woke up again an hour later, my skin was completely healed. To this day that skin condition has never returned. This was just another of the series of events that God used throughout my life to teach me, and to drive home the truth that the most important thing in life was my relationship with Him. Most of these life lessons I did not learn from books, but from the experiences of daily living.

Sometimes a bad experience can turn into a good one, especially if you can see it from God's perspective. For example, wrecking the old car that my father gave me was a setback that turned into a blessing. It caused me to purchase and use a bicycle, which not only provided me with a lot of time for prayer and worship as I rode back and forth to work, but also gave me plenty of exercise.

Another accident I was involved in had an even better outcome. One day, five of us were riding to church in a friend's car. We all were Bible students, and some, like me, were preachers. We had been studying together a book called Prison to Praise; its main theme was the importance of learning to praise God under any circumstances. At an intersection somewhere between Costa Mesa and Long Beach, the driver of a large van ran a red light and hit us broadside. Our car spun around, but did not overturn. Dazed and bleeding, many of us first thought, Is anyone dead? Are we all alive? Thankfully, none of us had sustained more than minor injuries—a major miracle, because the car was totaled.

With some difficulty, we pushed the doors open and got out of the car. By this time, the driver of the van, who was uninjured, had run over to check on us. "Oh, I am so sorry!" he said. "Are you all right? This is all my fault. I just had a big fight with my wife, and I was not concentrating on my driving. I did not even notice that red light. I feel just terrible about this."

There we were, five of us bleeding and standing in the middle of an intersection next to a demolished car, the driver of the other vehicle very apologetic, and a crowd of eyewitnesses gathering around us. We had recently been studying Prison to Praise, as well as hearing the lesson at school, "In everything, give praise to the Lord, in good things or bad things." Now we were in a position to put this teaching into practice.

"We were on our way to church," we told the van driver, "but obviously that's not going to happen now. Even though our car is demolished and we're all injured, the most important thing we want to know is, do you know the Lord?"

"I used to go to church," the man replied, "but I have not been there in a long time."

"Do you want to get right with the Lord?" I asked. "We can help you. We all are preachers or Bible school students, and we want you to know that God loves you. He wants to save you. All you have to do is trust Jesus Christ as your Lord and Savior."

"Can I?" he asked. "Is it that simple?"

"Yes, it is. Will you let us pray for you?"

"Yes."

We knelt down, right there in the middle of the intersection and prayed for this man. The people around us stared in amazement. "Is this an accident scene or a prayer meeting?" We prayed for the man, he gave his heart to Jesus, and we lifted up our voices in thanksgiving and praise to God because he got saved. "Thank You, Lord," we said. "We first did not know why You allowed this to happen, but now we understand Your reason."

After we finished praying, we all stood up and rejoiced with this man, who was so very happy that he had found the Lord.

Eventually, an ambulance came and took us to the hospital, where it was determined for sure that no one was seriously injured. They treated us, bandaged our wounds, and then released us. Because the other driver was at fault, his insurance company paid for the damages. Our friend, who owned the old car, was able to purchase a new car with the insurance money, and in addition, each of us received $1,000 in compensation for our injuries. For someone like me, who was going to Bible school and had no money, this was a small fortune. I felt like I had become rich overnight. What started out as a negative incident—a traffic accident—turned out to be a blessing for everyone. The other driver got saved, our friend received a new car, and we all got rich. Nobody lost anything—everybody gained!

One of the exciting things about the ministry of the Holy Spirit is watching how He carries out His own purposes, regardless of our personal agendas. This is why it is so important to be sensitive to the Spirit and ready to flow in whatever direction He is moving. I saw this over and over at Bethany Chapel. The church was heavily involved in street evangelism, and this too was a great opportunity for a young preacher in training like me to grow in the Lord and gain valuable experience.

I remember one day in 1964 we were holding a street meeting on Pacific Coast Boulevard in Long Beach, right down by the shore. We were having a great time, preaching, sharing the Gospel, and singing. Many people gathered around to watch and listen, whether from serious interest or idle curiosity. Either way, it did not matter; our goal was to preach the Word. At the end of each of these types of meetings, we would invite the audience to church for a time of refreshments, followed by another meeting in the evening. The church even provided a bus to transport any who wanted to come. Quite often, many of our listeners took us up on the offer.

At one point during this particular street meeting, one of the guys, who had been preaching in English, all of a sudden began speaking in tongues. None of us understood what he was saying, and he probably did not either. But just at that moment, a group of 15 to 20 sailors, who happened to be walking by right in front of him, stopped to listen. They all were in uniform, but were not American sailors. Some of us went over and tried to talk to them, but none of them could speak English. Nevertheless, they stood there and listened the whole time our colleague continued to preach in tongues.

After he finished speaking, the church bus pulled up, and without hesitation these international sailors climbed aboard. Some of us looked at each other and said, "How would they know to get on the bus when they don't understand English?" Nonetheless, we followed them onto the bus, and we all just sat there looking at each other. What else could we do? We could not communicate.

After we arrived at the church, we all climbed off the bus and went into the building. A lady there recognized the sailors' uniforms. "These are Greek sailors," she told us excitedly. "I know this because I, too, am from Greece." She went over to them and began talking to them in Greek. They seemed excited and very happy to find someone who could speak to them in their own language.

A little later she came back over to us. I could not contain my curiosity. "What's going on?" I asked. "What happened?"

She replied, "These fellows told me that they saw you on the street when they were walking by, but had no idea what you were doing. All of a sudden, they heard this American speaking to them in fluent Greek, and he even called them by name. He said to them, 'Jesus loves you,' and proceeded to share with them a very simple Gospel message, ending with the instruction, 'Stay here, because a bus will come to take you to a place where you can talk to someone in your own language.' "

Hence, the sailors knew to get on the bus even though they did not speak English. The Holy Spirit directed them, and they did what they were told. They came to the church, a woman from their own country witnessed to them in their language, and they all got saved.

Sometimes we think we know what the Holy Spirit is doing, but we need to be ready to adjust on a moment's notice when He starts moving in a direction different from what we have been expecting.

Another lesson I learned during my years at Bethany Chapel, is that if you consistently stand up for the Lord and preach the Gospel, eventually you will pay a price for your faith, even in America—the "land of the free." One day, we were preaching on the street when a couple of police officers stopped us. "You cannot preach on the streets; you are breaking the law. Do you have a permit?"

"No, we do not have a permit," we replied. "We didn't know we needed one."

Because we did not have a permit, they arrested us on the spot and took us to the police station. As it turned out, we did not have to go to jail. Instead, they gave us a citation and told us we were being charged with breaking the law. Later on, we were notified of a court date, when our case would be presented before a judge. Being young and still rather inexperienced, I did not know what to make of this development. How would this incident affect my future? I was a Bible student and a preacher in training who planned to go as a missionary to China. I certainly did not want to end up with a criminal record. What had I done wrong in the first place? I was just preaching. If I went to jail, I would not be able to finish my studies. These are the kinds of thoughts and feelings that were swirling through my head at the time.

Fortunately, we retained the services of a Christian attorney who was very good at his job and who accompanied us to court. He argued before the judge, on the basis of precedent of law in America, that in the United States of America, freedom of speech and freedom of religion were constitutionally protected liberties, and that people did not need a permit to preach anywhere in the country. He cited several precedents where similar arrests had happened to other people in other places, but the cases were dismissed and the defendants set free.

After listening to our attorney's arguments, the judge turned to the policemen who had arrested us and said, "First of all, I am going to release these defendants because they have broken no law, and second, I will give serious consideration to charging you with violating their civil rights." Then he dismissed the case against us, and we left, completely exonerated.

I like to tell this story whenever I go into China because it shows that opposition to the Gospel is not unique to a communist system. America is a free country, yet I was arrested there simply for preaching the Gospel on the street. I have also been arrested in China, but never for breaking the law or for any kind of criminal activity—only for preaching the Gospel. The irony is that even in China, with its communist government, there is no law against preaching the Gospel.

The incident of our arrest and release had an unexpected result. Instead of feeling intimidated, we became excited. "Wow! We got arrested and were taken to court! We got to suffer for the Lord!" This made us all the more bold. The next time a policeman or anyone else came up and tried to harass us for preaching the Gospel on the street, we were prepared. "You'd better make sure you know what you're doing," we cautioned respectfully. "The last people who harassed us for preaching almost got charged with violating our civil rights. You'd best leave us alone."

Sometimes the Holy Spirit works in ways we cannot possibly imagine. One day, some of us were at an amusement park in Long Beach passing out tracts. We were happy if even half the people we approached accepted one, and many of those who did simply threw them away. Before long, we were approached by a guy who looked really scary. He was big and tough, with well-developed muscles and tattoos all over his arms. Unsurprisingly, his black leather jacket identified him as a member of the Hell's Angels.

"What are you guys doing?" he demanded in a rough voice.

"We're just passing out tracts about Jesus," we answered, trying not to sound too intimidated.

"Really?" he said. "I want to do that! Give them to me."

Accordingly, we gave him all our tracts. What else could we do? He was a tough guy, and he had demanded them. We then watched in amazement as he walked up to one person after another, held out a tract, and said, "Take this!" People accepted them without question; I did not see a single person turn him down. After all, who would dare refuse to accept a tract from a member of the Hell's Angels?

In almost no time, he had passed out all the tracts, then turned to us and said, "Come with me to our headquarters. I want you to meet my boss."

We then followed him into the headquarters of the local Hell's Angels chapter. Gang members and groupies were lounging around, smoking, drinking, passed out in a dead drunk, and some having sex. We then entered another room where our guide introduced us to another man, and said, "This is the boss of our local chapter. I want you to talk to him."

The whole experience seemed so unreal, so improbable, that we knew it had to be of the Lord. So we began to talk to him about Christ. He said, "I know I'm a sinner. I'm tired of this life. If I keep going the way I'm going, I know I will die before long. Can I get saved?"

"Sure you can," I said. We prayed for him, and he accepted the Lord. It really was that simple. Talk about a heart that was ready to receive the Gospel!

After giving his heart to Christ, this tough gang leader asked, "When can I be baptized?"

It so happened that it was a Sunday evening. So he came with us to church that night, and he was baptized. Sometimes you don't know whose heart the Holy Spirit is working on; that is why it is so important to be sensitive and watch to see where He is moving.

Even though I had been called to be a missionary to China, I did not want to wait until I got to China to be a missionary. I started immediately right there at home. Nor was I going to limit my preaching to church meetings; I wanted to get out where the people were living life. Christian conferences and sessions were important for my training, but I was eager to be out where there were no Christians. I was around Christians all the time at church. I wanted to go where the world was, where there was sin, a place where I could let my light shine and really help people. So, we regularly went into bars, sex establishments, theaters—anywhere we could meet people who needed the Lord. We preached on street corners and sometimes even on public buses. Our passion was to tell as many people as we could about Jesus, whenever and wherever we found them.

In addition, I was still always interested in confirming signs that would encourage and help strengthen my conviction of being called to China. During one meeting, shortly after I began attending Bethany Chapel, Pastor David Schoch called me up to prophesy over me. There were several other prophetic men in that meeting as well, none of whom knew me very well. Some of them had never even met me personally before that meeting. Nevertheless, they begin to prophesy over me. One of them said, "I see, regarding this young man, that God has called him into full-time ministry."

I was listening intently to all their words, of course, as well as praying to the Lord in my spirit at the same time. I was hungry for a more complete revelation to further confirm what I already knew in my heart, so I prayed, "Lord, give them more revelation."

Another of the prophets said, "Yes, in fact, I see that this young man is going to be a missionary. He is going to leave the United States and go overseas."

That was indeed more revelation, but I still was not satisfied. "Lord, give them more revelation."

A third man said, "I see this young man ministering to people who have yellow skin and black hair. They are Asian people."

Wonderful! I thought. Asian people! Even so, I knew that there were Filipinos, Koreans, and Japanese, as well as Chinese.

Then David Schoch prophesied, "I see that this young man is going to go to Red China." This was amazing, because there was no way he could have known this except by revelation from the Lord. He continued, revealing certain matters word for word that I had prayed to the Lord, but had shared with no one else.

These prophetic words certainly brought the confirmation I had been seeking, but they did even more; they also released spiritual gifts into my life. From that time on, I began to prophesy; and after that, other gifts of the Spirit came to me—gifts of healing, and words of knowledge.

I will always be deeply thankful to the Lord for placing me, during the formative years of my ministry, in a church that so thoroughly honored the Holy Spirit. The experiences I had and the lessons I learned shaped the approach to ministry that I have followed for over 40 years. They also prepared me for the next phase of my life—military service and a year in Vietnam at the height of the war.

CHAPTER SEVEN
FIGHTING FOR JESUS

All in all, I spent nearly four years at Bethany Chapel—critical and formative years. During that time, I received priceless training in preparation of fulfilling the call God had placed on my life. I went to every meeting I could possibly attend, paid attention to a lot of powerful biblical preaching, and witnessed the Holy Spirit moving in power more times than I could number. I enrolled in the church's Bible training school, devoured the Word of God, and grabbed every opportunity to preach that came my way. I was so hungry to study, to learn, and to grow.

One of the activities I enjoyed most was the evangelistic outreach we conducted every Friday night. We would preach and share the Gospel on streets, in bars, at amusement parks, on the beach—anywhere we could. At one point, though, sadly enough, this became an issue that threatened to divide the church.

There was one group in the church to whom God had given a powerful prophetic anointing and many accurate words of knowledge. For a time, this was very beneficial, because the ministry of this group helped to build and strengthen the Body of Christ. Unfortunately, they gradually drifted away from the truth and succumbed to pride, believing they were more "spiritual" than anyone else in the church, including Pastor Schoch. They claimed that they alone could truly hear the voice of the Lord. This group even began holding their own private prayer meetings, where they received all sorts of revelation and prophecies, saw visions (even of angels), and prayed for the rest of us "carnal" folks.

In the meantime, I was most interested in saving the lost and bringing others to Jesus. It wasn't long before this group, however, received a "revelation" that our Friday night excursions to preach the Gospel were carnal and of the flesh. "You need to listen to the voice of the Lord," they would say. "If He wants you to go to the amusement park and preach, only then do you go. Otherwise, He may not want you to do that. Just stay back and have a prayer meeting or a Bible study."

"That's crazy!" I responded. "I don't have to pray about whether I should preach the Gospel or not. Jesus said to go and preach the Gospel." I believed that then, and I believe it still. "There are some things you don't have to pray about," I continued, "because the Lord has already told us to do them. Preaching the Gospel is one of them. I might pray about how to preach, or exactly which location to go to, but I don't have to pray about whether or not to preach the Gospel. That is a given."

They were not convinced. "You are so unspiritual," they declared. "You are doing this in the flesh, and it is carnal."

"What could be 'carnal' about preaching the Gospel?" I asked them. They didn't have an answer.

The problem became so severe that I finally went to Pastor David Schoch. Surprisingly, despite his prophetic gift, he was not aware of the friction. Pastor Schoch was wise in the ways of the Lord and mature in spirit, and he dealt with the situation in time to prevent a church split. It was a difficult time, because the leader of this divisive group had also been placed in a leadership position in the church by Pastor Schoch himself. In the aftermath, this leader left the church, taking with him his group of followers, which numbered several dozen. The last I heard of them, which was many years ago, they had drifted into deep error, becoming a cult. To this day, I continue to believe that we must always make preaching the Gospel our number-one priority.

Toward the end of my involvement with Bethany Chapel, Pastor Schoch gave another prophecy concerning me that was even more amazing than the first prophecy.

By 1966, America's military involvement in Vietnam, which began under President Kennedy and expanded under President Johnson, was well underway. At that time, the military draft (to be later abolished in the early 1970s by President Nixon in favor of an all-volunteer force) was a major source for filling the ranks of America's armed forces. And like other young men my age, I registered for the draft at the age of 18, in accordance with federal law. Depending on how many inductees were needed by whatever segment of the military at any given time, and on how many young men were living in a particular location, a man might be called up immediately, or deferred for a year or two, or not called up at all. Usually, any male who reached the age of 21 without being drafted could breathe easier, because being called up at that age or later became increasingly unlikely.

Even though I obeyed the law and registered for the draft at age 18, I had no desire to go into the military. The war in Vietnam was heating up, and I knew that if I was drafted, I would probably be sent there. I did not want to go to Vietnam. It was not a matter of courage or the lack of it. I wanted to be a missionary to China, and was not interested in anything that would distract me from that goal. Little did I know how God was about to work in my life.

As my 21st birthday approached, I became more and more confident that I had escaped the draft…I was wrong. On April 3, 1966—my 21st birthday—I received a letter from the federal government, signed by President Johnson, ordering me to report to a specific induction center on a specific date for service in the United States Army. My report date was only a couple weeks away. The letter went on to state that refusal to report would result in criminal prosecution. I did not want to go into the Army, but neither did I want to go to jail. In the end, I really had no choice; I would report for duty as ordered.

Before I left, Pastor Schoch prophesied over me. I had told him that I had been drafted, and the prophecy he received had to do with my upcoming military service. "When you go into the military, even when you go to Vietnam, God will be with you and God will protect you. You will go and you will come back, because God is going to send you to Red China to preach the Gospel." His final words are the ones that really stuck with me: "Not one hair of your head will be harmed. Men may fall on your left side, and on your right side, but not one hair of your head will be harmed."

Imagine the comfort those words brought to a young man, who knew that he probably would be heading off to war! Knowing Pastor Schoch's stellar track record of accuracy in prophetic words, I was confident that I could trust what he had told me. Besides, I also had the witness of the Holy Spirit in my spirit that this was so.

When the day of my induction arrived, I reported to the designated place, boarded a bus with a bunch of other guys who had also been drafted, and was taken to the induction center. There we were led into a large room and told to wait. A few minutes later, an Army sergeant entered the room. "Gentlemen, whether you like it or not, whether you think it fortunate or unfortunate, you are being drafted into the United States Army. I'm going to be very honest with you—this is the law. Many of you will be sent to Vietnam, and, probably, not a few of you will die there. But you do have a choice. If you do not want to join the Army, and possibly end up in Vietnam, in a few minutes I'll ask you to raise your hand, and we will take you into another room, charge you with noncompliance with the Selective Service law, and you will probably spend the next five years in prison. If, however, you comply with the law, as a draftee you will be making only a two-year commitment to the Army. We will take you into another room in a few minutes and swear you in. From that moment on, until your two-year tour of duty is up, you will be in the Army."

The advantage of the draft was that it was only a two-year commitment, as opposed to four years for those who joined up voluntarily. On the other hand, volunteers could choose their branch of the service as well as their specific job. Draftees had no choice; they were assigned strictly according to need. The Army decided what you would do, and in those days during the escalation of the war in

Vietnam, 90 percent of draftees ended up in the infantry.

Given the choice of military service or prison, perhaps one or two in the room chose the option of refusing the draft. Everyone there was in his late teens or early 20s, and in many ways our lives were just beginning. To most of us, a two-year stint in the Army with the probability of Vietnam duty, and the possibility of death seemed preferable to the certainty of five years in prison for refusing military service.

Subsequently, we were led into another room and informed that due to personnel losses in Vietnam they needed to draft people for the Marines as well as for the Army. However, instead of giving us the option of volunteering for the Marines, they lined us up and counted us off by sixes. Every sixth man was selected to go into the Marines.

This really worried me. Being drafted into the Army was bad enough, but to end up in the Marines would have been even worse. The Marines had the toughest, harshest, and most rigorous training program of all the services. They were among the most disciplined and well-trained military forces in the world, and they were always assigned to the most dangerous missions. I felt I could handle the Army for two years, but feared I would never make it as a Marine. So as we were lined up for the count off, I prayed, "Lord, I will never make it in the Marines. Please have mercy; make it possible for me to go into the Army." As I stood there praying, they counted us off: One, two, three, four... then they came to me. Five! I was number five! The guy standing to my left was number six, and he was pulled from the line for the Marines. In my heart I was praising God. I had missed going into the Marines by one count. Had I simply stood a few inches to the left, I would have ended up in the Marines... and probably would not have survived.

I was now officially in the Army. This was the first of many mercies that the Lord showed to me over the next couple of years. A second one came just a few hours later.

After we were sworn in, we were escorted immediately to the airport to fly to Fort Bliss, Texas for basic training. We did not fly out of Los Angeles International Airport, but departed from a much smaller military airfield on a Lockheed L188 turboprop. We all climbed aboard, found our seats, and the plane took off. Then about an hour into the flight, we received our first shock—one of the turboprop engines caught fire. I was sitting right beside the wing and watched it happen. Needless to say, I became quite concerned! To make matters worse, the plane then ran into some really bad turbulence. Thousands of feet in the air, an engine on fire, bouncing up and down violently— it felt like the aircraft was about to shake apart at any moment.

All around me, guys were crying out, "We're going to die! We're going to die!" Some of them started praying, and others started cursing. It seemed that everybody on board that plane was terrified… everybody except me. Don't get me wrong. I am no more heroic by nature than anyone else, but I had something going for me that most, if not all, of the other men on that plane did not. Godly prophecies had been spoken over me…I would go to China as a missionary and God would protect me—"…not one hair of my head would be harmed."

I knew the airplane was in trouble, but I also knew that I was not going to die, and that probably no one else would either. I was so certain that the Lord's hand of protection was upon me that even if the plane did crash and everyone else on board died, I would still walk away. My confidence in God and His promises gave me peace in the midst of this storm. And during those terrifying moments I realized, This is a great time to witness! So I started talking to the guys around me.

"What will happen to you, if you die?" I asked one of them. "Will you go to Heaven or to hell?"

"I'll probably go to hell," he replied.

At least he was being honest. "Do you want to go to Heaven?"

"Sure."

So I prayed for him and led him to the Lord. Then the guy in front of me said, "Can I go to Heaven too?" Even today, I always get a laugh when I tell people that the best time to witness is when you are on a plane that is going to crash. Everybody wants to be prayed for. Everybody wants to hear the Gospel then.

I prayed with several guys, absolutely confident that everything was going to be all right. And in the end it was. The fire went out, the turbulence stopped, and the plane landed safely. As I exited the plane, I noticed the pilot examining the damaged engine, which was leaking oil. He shook his head with doubt, and the look on his face seemed to communicate, "This plane is not going to make it much longer." Indeed, his concern was justified.

Years later, I learned that the very next day that very same airplane crashed, killing 83 soldiers. I did some research on the Lockheed L188 and discovered that throughout its history this particular aircraft model had crashed 47 times, causing the death of 1,041 people. You would think that when a plane had crashed that many times, it would have been removed from service long before it would become responsible for so many casualties. Actually, it was seldom used for civilian passengers, but mostly by the military.

I flew on that plane on April 21, 1966, and it crashed on April 22. Just as one number had placed me into the Army instead of the Marines, so had just one day separated me from probable death in a plane crash. The Lord was watching out for me and protecting me, along with all the other men on that plane. Nothing would thwart God's plan for me, or sidetrack His call on my life.

After completing basic training at Fort Bliss, I was assigned to the First Air Cavalry and stationed at the Presidio, which was located next to the Golden Gate Bridge in San Francisco. Despite its name, the First Air Cavalry was actually an infantry outfit that was supported by helicopters, particularly the heavy, twin-rotored Chinooks and the smaller Huey gunships. Because my records showed that I had worked as a cook in a university dining hall, the Army also assigned me as a cook. Although I was in the infantry, my specific job was preparing meals for the division. This worked out great for me, because I was on duty only in the morning and the afternoon; I had every evening free. The Chinese have a saying, "You ride a cow to find a horse," meaning that you accept your circumstances in the meantime while you are waiting and hoping for something better. You are willing to take a temporary job before you are able to find employment in your preferred career. That was my attitude while in the Army. My goal was to be a missionary to the Chinese, and being a cook in the Army was simply a stepping-stone to that goal—I was riding a cow until I could get a horse.

The Presidio was one of the best Army camps in America. A completely open post, it operated on something almost like the honor system; you didn't have to check in or check out. Even today it is the same way. I liked the fact that the Presidio was located in an especially nice area—very scenic and very old. And it was while stationed there that I became involved with Shiloh Church, the church that later sponsored my move to Hong Kong as a missionary and has continued to support me throughout the years.

After I had served in the Army for six months, I was subsequently posted to Vietnam for a one-year tour. Most of that time was spent in advanced camps and firebases that were often in close proximity to the Viet Cong. I became quite familiar with the sounds of small arms fire, artillery, and mortars, as well as the staccato bursts of machine guns and the whoosh of rockets from the gunships. Rarely did a night go by without the sound of fighting. However, although I was surrounded by warfare, I refused to fight, not because I was a coward or unpatriotic, but because I understood that my purpose was not to bring death, but life through the Gospel of Christ, even in Vietnam. If any of my buddies in the unit would have ever gotten into a bind where their lives would have been seriously threatened unless I acted, I would have fought to defend and protect them; but I would not deliberately seek to take a life, not even of the enemy.

For example, when we often flew in helicopters on low-level missions over fields and jungles, someone would man the machine guns in the open doors of the choppers, spraying the ground below in order to prevent sniper fire. Yet I refused to do so because I did not want to kill anybody. Instead, I sat inside and attended to other tasks.

My main focus, even in Vietnam, was preaching the Gospel and witnessing for Christ, which I did wherever I could and as often as I could. I found a local Christian Missionary Alliance Church where I frequently picked up a load of tracts to hand out. Then I would go into the Buddhist temples, or walk up to people on the streets, hand them a tract, and say, "God sent me here as a missionary. I'm not here to fight anybody's war, except the war for Jesus Christ." I had a great time doing that, and along the way, I even learned to speak a little Vietnamese.

Even today I often travel to Vietnam on ministry trips. The CMA church that had supplied me with those tracts is long gone, however, supplanted, as with all the other churches in the country, by the state church sanctioned by the communist Vietnamese government.

In the field, in the outlying firebases, we lived in shelters made of sandbags. We also dug trenches in the ground, which became our refuge whenever enemy fire became too intense and dangerous for us to stay in the shelters. During these times, captured Vietcong prisoners would pass through our camps on a fairly regular basis. They would be captured during or after a firefight, confined behind barbed wire set up around a special section of the camp, and then moved out soon after. Anytime I saw a group of these prisoners, I would pray for them and try to witness to them. If I was able to talk to them (and often I was not), I would say words like, "Don't be afraid, your problem is going to be solved. God loves you." To me, every person I saw was someone who needed Jesus. It did not matter which side of the conflict they were on.

I also looked for ways to help the local Vietnamese people. As an Army cook, I knew that we always had extra food left over after mess that was simply thrown away. "Let's take the leftover food and give it to the people," I suggested.

"Oh, you can't do that," I was told. "It's too dangerous. We don't know who these people are. They may be Viet Cong in disguise." That was a possibility. We all had heard of soldiers who had been killed by Viet Cong disguised as village peasants.

"Well, that is a risk, of course," I acknowledged, "but at the same time, we could do some good." The welfare of the people was always on my heart, and besides, I feared no personal harm because of God's promise to protect me. It was through this ministry that the Lord created a love within me for the Asian people. The Vietnamese people are very much like the Chinese, and the Vietnamese language is very similar to the Cantonese that we speak in Hong Kong.

Despite my commitment not to fight or to kill, as an infantryman I was required to carry a weapon whenever we went on patrol. In fact, I carried two. My principal weapon was an M-79 grenade launcher, a single-shot weapon that could fire a high-explosive shell a maximum distance of 350 meters. It was very dangerous at close range, so soldiers never used it for close distances. The M-79 was more of a psychological weapon among the troops, because they felt isolated and exposed at the outlying fire bases. The grenade from the M-79 had to travel at least 15 feet before it activated. But even at that distance, if it exploded, the firer and those around him could get hit with shrapnel. For that reason, every soldier who carried an M-79 also carried a 45-caliber pistol for close-range combat.

Even though I was required to carry a weapon, I refused to carry ammunition. When some of my superiors challenged me regarding this choice, I explained, "I'm not here to kill anybody. The Lord sent me to preach the Gospel. I'm not going to fight in this war; I'm going to fight in the war of Jesus. But if the enemy is coming and your life is in danger, I will consider helping you…but I'm really not planning to do that. I believe God is going to protect me."

This really upset them. One officer told me, "You can't do this. We will court-martial you."

"Do whatever you want," I replied, "but I'm not going to kill anyone."

They wanted to court-martial me, but were unable to do so because of a technicality. The Army handbook for soldiers said that every soldier had to carry a weapon, but nowhere did it state that a soldier had to carry ammunition. Technically, I was in compliance with Army regulations, so there was nothing they could do. Finally, they let it go. The officer who originally threatened me with court-martial eventually said, "Let's just forget about it. We're all here for only a year, anyway. We know you're here just to preach the Gospel; you do what you want to do, and we'll do what we want to do." And that was the end of it.

We would conduct patrols quite often, and the Lord was so good to me. Each time, I would pray in tongues and worship the Lord; and whenever I could, in camp or on patrol, I would witness to the other guys. Many of them could not have cared less about God and had no desire to follow Him—not, at least, until they came under heavy fire and thought they were about to die. The old adage that there are no atheists in fox holes is true. I saw even some of the most hardened, God-cursing men calling out to Him in terror as bullets whizzed by inches above their heads and shells exploded all around them. In those times I wanted to shout, "Don't you think it's a little bit late right now? You have been rejecting God all your life, and now you want Him to help you?" But I knew how merciful God is, so instead of berating them, I would simply say, "You need to give your life to Him right now."

One day a strange notion entered my head. I am so close to China, I thought, that maybe I can just go to China from here. So I grabbed a compass and left the camp, heading north, in the direction of China. Looking back on it now, I realize it was a stupid thing to do. First of all, I would have been considered a deserter, and would have lived under the cloud of being a fugitive from military justice. Secondly, had I kept going, I probably never would have survived. Even as I walked north, there were times when I could see the bushes on either side of me moving, which meant that there were people hiding there, probably Viet Cong. Even in this foolish decision, the Lord protected me, because no one came out. I was never attacked.

After walking for about two hours, and covering perhaps two or three miles, the Lord spoke to me very clearly: "Go back. I'm going to take you to China, but this is not the way. Your experience in Vietnam will help you to get there, but now is not the time. Be patient. Trust Me, and you will be in China a few years from now." So I went back to camp. I didn't tell anybody what I had done, because they probably would have thought I was crazy, not to mention that I could've been arrested for attempted desertion. In my youth and immaturity, my call to China felt so real to me and so compelling, that I thought that maybe the Lord would use my presence in Vietnam to get me into

China. In retrospect, I am so glad I waited…for all kinds of reasons.

Because of the prophecies that had been spoken over me, my continual awareness of God's presence with me, and His protective hand on my life, I had a different take on the war than most of the people I served with. For instance, I kept telling everyone that America was going to lose the war. Again, this was not because I was unpatriotic or a pessimist, but because of another prophecy. Before I had left the United States, Pastor David Schoch prophesied that America would lose the war. Because I had great respect for his track record of prophetic accuracy, I put more stock in his words than in any pronouncements that came out of the White House or the Pentagon. The official line was there was no way we could lose—we had all sorts of advanced weaponry that the North Vietnamese did not have—napalm, infrared night vision that could spot the enemy on even the darkest of nights, and "smart" bombs that could alter course in mid-flight and take out the enemy whenever he tried to flee into places such as a building or a cave.

Despite all this advanced technology, however, the United States did indeed lose the war…for many reasons. Bureaucrats and leaders half a world away in Washington tried to micromanage the war rather than allow the commanders on the field the free hand they needed to get the job done. This factor also contributed to the increasing unpopularity of the war at home. Another reason for the failure was the generally poor quality of American soldiers in Vietnam, particularly many of the draftees who had been hippies before the war—who rejected the discipline, and refused to respect authority and the chain of command that is so vital for military success.

I remember one day, when Viet Cong were spotted in a nearby field only a few hundred feet away, a sergeant ordered his men to rush them and take them out. But instead of following his command, they spitefully responded, "You go first; we'll follow you." In many cases there simply was no discipline. This impacted me personally. I had been in Vietnam only one month when an enemy mortar round struck the mess tent, killing an entire crew of cooks—all my superiors, in fact. So, one month into my tour in Vietnam, I suddenly found myself promoted to sergeant. Often I would give an order to those under my command, yet they would disregard it. Rather than fight what I thought was a losing battle, I ended up doing the job myself. After all, who cared? We were there for only a year anyway.

Despite the almost daily assault of gunfire, artillery, and mortar fire that fell on our camp, I survived my year in Vietnam without a scratch, just as the Lord had promised. Although I had been no braver by nature than anyone else, my certainty of His protective hand had given me a boldness and confidence in the face of danger, which I probably otherwise would not have had.

At one time, the Viet Cong somehow managed to surround our camp in a valley near Cambodia by positioning themselves in the mountains all around us. That night, they began lobbing grenades and firing mortars and machine guns into the camp. They would use tracer bullets, where every seventh bullet would light up, allowing them to direct their line of fire more accurately at nighttime.

As big lines of bullets continued to be fired and mortar bursts erupted all over the camp, we all remained hunkered down in our hooches, the little huts we had built out of sandbags. The problem was that the generator that powered the lights was located in the center of the camp, away from everything else. Lights were brightly lit all over the camp, so that the Viet Cong could see everything clearly from the hillside. And as long as the lights stayed on, we were sitting ducks. Someone needed to turn off the generator, but the enemy barrage was so fierce that no one dared step out into the open. To make the attempt would have seemed suicidal.

Nevertheless, I knew the Lord had promised to protect me, so I decided to go for it. Confident that I was safe in God's hands, I walked calmly from my hut down the hill to the generator and shut it down. Immediately the camp was doused in pitch darkness. Consequently, the barrage ceased because the Vietcong could no longer see their target. My actions were not particularly heroic; I was simply a young man who knew I was safe under the protective hand of God. My destiny was to go to China, not to die on a field in Vietnam.

Afterwards, when I became a little hungry, I grabbed some food from the mess before I went back to my hut. Normally, at least two soldiers shared a hut, but I had one to myself. No one had wanted to stay with me because I was always reading my Bible, praying, and trying to talk to them about the Lord. But all of a sudden, some of the guys came crawling up. I guess they were afraid the enemy might start firing again. "Can we stay here beside you?" they asked.

"Why?" I responded.

"We have seen how God protects you. Nothing happened to you. That was really brave."

"It wasn't brave," I said. "It's just that I know that God is with me."

"Well, we think that if we stay next to you, maybe God will protect us too."

It was as though they thought there was some kind of supernatural aura of protection around me that they could get inside.

"It's okay with me if you stay here," I said, "but I'm going to preach the Gospel to you guys."

"That's okay," they assured me. "We'll put up with that, if we can just stay here with you."

They stayed in the hut with me for several hours, and I shared the Lord with them.

Another time, I was at work when I suddenly heard the Lord say to me very clearly, "Get up and leave this area." Instead of finishing my job, I listened to the Lord's warning and immediately walked away.

"Where are you going?" some of the others asked.

"The Lord told me to leave."

Three minutes later, a mortar round landed on the exact spot where I had been working. Had I stayed there, I would have been dead.

A Christian buddy of mine had his own experience of God's protection. He once boarded a military plane to fly from an army base in the field to Saigon. There had been open seating on the plane, and as he boarded he heard the Lord say to him very clearly, "Don't sit in the back. Sit next to the door." He wasn't sure why the Lord told him to do this, but he obeyed, and took a seat beside the door. As the plane shot down the runway, for some reason it did not have enough power to complete the takeoff, yet the pilot waited too long to abort the flight. The plane overshot the runway and then plowed into some trees. My friend, who had been sitting right next the door, simply kicked it open and jumped out of the plane. A few seconds later, the plane exploded and everyone else on board died. My friend was the only survivor, and he survived only because he had sat beside the door, just as the Lord had told him to do.

At another time, I had to make a special trip to a place called "Sin City." I previously mentioned that one of the weapons I carried was a 45 caliber semiautomatic pistol, but I had no holster for it. Things like pistol holsters and other such items would be shipped over from the United States but would somehow fall into the hands of a Vietnamese official, or even a corrupt American military member who was lining his pockets on the side. They would not steal weapons, because that was too dangerous, but they frequently took supplies.

Because the 45 caliber pistol was fairly heavy, I knew I needed a holster to carry it. So I asked the supply clerks where I could purchase one.

"You can get one in 'Sin City,' " they replied.

"Sin City" was the American nickname for a city in the northern part of South Vietnam that was known for drugs and prostitution. I had never had any reason to go there—until now. I needed a holster, and apparently Sin City was the place to get it. Interestingly, when I proceeded to leave the post, the guy at the checkout desk asked me if I had any condoms.

"Why do I need condoms?" I asked.

"Because there are a lot of prostitutes there."

"That has nothing to do with me," I replied. "I'm just going to buy a holster."

He was not convinced. It was his experience that American soldiers going to Sin City were always looking for prostitutes and needed condoms to prevent catching a disease.

"I'm a Christian. I don't do things like that," I insisted.

He told me of a couple other soldiers who were Christians also, yet had taken condoms and visited prostitutes in the city. I checked them out later. One had a girlfriend in the States, and the other had a wife and young child. Although they were believers, they were not Spirit-filled. They did not pray in the Spirit or worship in the Spirit, and so did not have the inner moral strength to resist temptation.

When you pray in the Holy Spirit, when you love the Lord, and love His Word, there is an inner strength in you that helps you walk in purity and holiness and righteousness.

After arguing back and forth with the guy for several minutes, he finally let me go without the condoms. And I went to Sin City and bought the holster. Afterward, as I continued to walk down the street, I happened to pass one of the local sex establishments. Several attractive young Vietnamese women who worked at the brothel smiled at me, began talking to me, and invited me inside. I accepted their offer and went inside, but not for the reason they had expected. To their surprise, I immediately pulled out my Bible and started talking to them about Jesus. After a few minutes, they informed me that they had business to conduct, and if I was not there to do that type of business with them, I had to leave. So they threw me out.

I simply walked into another establishment and did the same thing. I visited three or four "businesses" and took the opportunity in each one to preach the Gospel. When I returned to the base, the same guy I had talked to earlier asked me if I had been to see the prostitutes.

"Well, I saw them," I said, "but I don't think they liked me very much. And I can't figure out why."

It was activities like these for which I gained the nickname "Preacher" from the other guys in my unit. Many of them used it in a mocking way, but I didn't care. After all, I was a preacher. That was my calling, and my heart. I may have been a U.S. soldier in the midst of a war against the communist North Vietnamese, but I was fighting for Jesus.

As for an assigned spiritual leader, there had been a chaplain in our unit, but I soon discovered that he was very liberal and actually was not even born again. He did not believe in Heaven or hell, or that the Bible was true and was the Word of God. So I started an informal church with some of the other guys. We met together for prayer, worship, Bible study, and preaching. We witnessed many miracles, and quite a few men came to the Lord. In particular, we once prayed for one young soldier, a lieutenant, who was in danger of losing one of his legs from a badly infected wound. And the Lord healed him completely.

During the year that I was in Vietnam, I was often in danger's way...but never was even one hair on my head harmed. Any number of times I could have been a target, especially when I went into the towns or villages, but the Lord always protected me. By the time I left Vietnam, most of the 120 men in my original platoon had either been killed or wounded. God's protection of me was so complete that to this day I believe I was just about the only man in my unit who never received the Purple Heart, which is awarded to every military member who is wounded in combat or as a direct result of enemy action.

Midway through my tour in Vietnam, I went to Hong Kong on R & R, which I previously described in the Prologue of this book. After my R & R in Hong Kong, I returned to Vietnam, finished my tour, and was rotated back to the United States. When I returned stateside, I still had six months to serve in order to finish out my two-year enlistment. Initially, I was slated to go to an Army base in Georgia, but I really wanted to return to the West Coast, specifically, as close as possible to the San Francisco area so I could visit Shiloh Church, where I had previously attended for several months before going to Vietnam. At that church they had been so open to the work of the Holy Spirit and also involved in evangelism and compassionate ministry to street people, including many of the hippies. Shiloh was just a small church at that time, smaller than Bethany Chapel; but during the year that I was in Vietnam, many people in the church wrote to me. They continually prayed for me and kept in touch. Sister Violet Kiteley, the pastor, really loved me.

Fortunately for me, one of my uncles worked at the Presidio in San Francisco. Upon returning stateside, I had a few days leave before I was to report to Georgia, and I called Uncle Dewey to ask if he could do anything to make it possible for me to stay in the general

San Francisco area. Subsequently, he made a call to the Pentagon and arranged for me to be stationed at Fort Ord, in Monterey, California, a couple of hours drive south of San Francisco. Interestingly enough, Monterey also has a military base called the Presidio, which today is the home of the U.S. military's Defense Language Institute.

When I arrived at Fort Ord, I bought a brand-new 1968 Volkswagen Beetle for $1800, with money I had managed to save. In one year, I drove that car more than 50,000 miles going back and forth to Shiloh. I never missed a single meeting or Bible study, and would always take people to church with me, usually guys from the base.

Six months after returning from Vietnam, I was then discharged from the Army, and six months after that, I felt it was time to go to China. The call had always been strong, and the ten days of R & R in Hong Kong had whetted my appetite all the more. Sister Kiteley also knew of my call, so I went to her and said, "It's time for me to go to China."

"This is a very small church," she said. "I don't know if we can support you."

"Listen," I replied, "I've brought a few dozen people to this church already; their tithes should be at least enough to get me a one-way ticket."

"Well," she continued, "we're not sure if you're ready."

"Pastor," I responded, "you are always telling us that Jesus is coming soon. If you wait any longer, Jesus will come back, and I will never get to go."

I finally convinced her. The church paid for a one-way airline ticket for me, and I flew to Hong Kong in March 1969. The next phase of my life was about to begin, the phase for which God had been preparing me for nearly 24 years.

Featured in Charisma magazine – 1994

Dennis and his siblings –
Roxanna, Doug, Patti, Cheryl,
Bruce, and Jeannine

Dennis –
the oldest
of seven

Dennis in Vietnam – 1966

The Christian soldier who
only came to save lives —
no bullets in his gun

The Army Commendation Medal

Kathy — number 3 of 4 children (Keith, Stan, Kathy, and Evelyn)

Dennis and Kathy's wedding on Dennis' 26th birthday – April 3, 1971

On the way to the reception

*On the ministry trail
during our honeymoon –
Kathy at the piano*

*On the ministry trail –
Dennis sharing
about China*

*Dennis and Kathy with
Donna, Dennis' mother, at
the San Francisco airport –
Being sent off to Hong Kong
– May 1971*

Being released to Hong Kong with a blessing – Dennis' parents, Clayton & Donna, and Kathy's parents, Lewis and Florence, and other Shiloh church members

Hong Kong pastors, church leaders, and some church members at a network meeting in Hong Kong – 1972

Church service at our church on Mody Road, located near Hong Kong Christian College – late 1970s

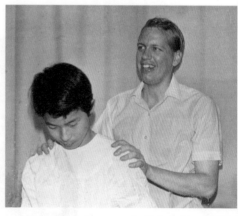

And the church grew as the Holy Spirit added many precious people – water baptism at Revival Christian Church, Hong Kong

He enthrones the praises of His people – Revival Christian Church, Hong Kong – 1978

After teaching on "David's Tabernacle," they organized a band to surprise Dennis – 1987

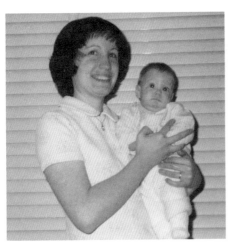

Our beautiful firstborn – Sharon Grace – 1973

Sharon and her dad – 1979

Sharon and her baby brother, Michael – 1976

Such fun!

The Balcombe family – 1976

Having a typical Chinese family meal

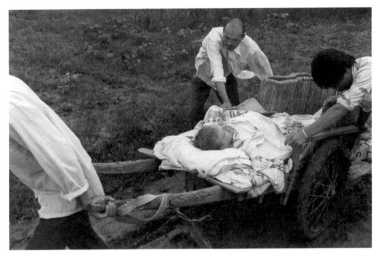

Into the villages of China - Dennis taken in as a "corpse" – 1980s

Traveling with Chinese brothers and sisters – 1980s

Traveling to a house church leadership meeting - Henan Province – Late 1980s

Praying for house church leaders to receive the Baptism of the Holy Spirit – Late 1980s

Dennis & Kathy at the new Revival Christian Church location, Hong Kong – 1983

Samuel Lau married Sharon in 1995

Precious hand-copied Bibles for the house church in China – we began to carry in Bibles in 1979

The house church of China met together in the village homes

"Let the little children come unto Me" – Revival Christian Church, Hong Kong – 1997

Revival Christian Church meeting – Most of the congregation were students from two middle schools, 1980-1982

Samuel, Sharon, Kady Joy,
and Benjamin Peace Lau – 2001

The Balcombe & Lau families – 2006

Our Pastors from our home church, Shiloh, joined us to celebrate Revival Christian
Church's 40th Anniversary – (L to R) Pastor Violet Kiteley, Pastors Dennis & Kathy,
Pastors David & Marilyn Kiteley, Pastors Patrick & Marlena Kiteley

Presently, Revival Christian Church, Hong Kong, 2011

PART 2

CHAPTER EIGHT
BECOMING CHINESE

I arrived in Hong Kong with very little money—50 or maybe 100 dollars—and an open-ended commitment of support from Shiloh Church in Oakland. Because they were a small church in those days, I knew I could depend on only a small amount of financial assistance—perhaps as much as a hundred dollars a month. Yet the amount really did not matter to me; I was simply overjoyed and encouraged that they believed enough in me and in my call to China to support me at all. The greatest support they gave me was their promise to pray for me regularly. This was of utmost importance because I wanted to be under legitimate spiritual covering as I began the work for which God had been preparing me all my life. Even more importantly, I knew God was with me and would protect and provide for me. What was there to worry about?

Previously, my only point of contact in Hong Kong had been Paul Collins, who had met with me and prophesied over me during my R & R two years before. When I arrived in Hong Kong in March 1969, however, Paul Collins was no longer there; he had returned to Australia. Instead, I had been given the name and address of an American missionary, Kay Locke, who worked with drug addicts in Hong Kong. "Look her up when you get to Hong Kong," I was advised, "and she will give you good advice for getting settled in and starting your work."

So once again, here I was in Hong Kong; and like before, I arrived with little more than a few dollars in my pocket and the name of a contact person. But this time, there was a major difference. In 1967, I had visited for ten days and had a guaranteed free flight back to my unit in Vietnam. Now, two years later, I was here to stay. For better or for worse, I was "stuck" in Hong Kong. Even if I had wanted to leave, I didn't have enough money for an airplane or boat ticket to return home.

But I did not want to leave. I had been waiting for this day all my life. Hong Kong! I was here at last, not for a brief visit, but to invest my life. It felt so wonderful to be back in this great city! As I took a cab from the airport, once again I soaked in the sights, sounds, and smells. A strange and wonderful awareness suddenly swept over me...I was home! There awoke in me a dawning sense of kinship with the teeming masses of people I saw all around me going about their daily affairs. Although I was a blonde-haired, blue-eyed, fair-skinned "foreigner" from America who could speak only a few words of Cantonese, my heart was already becoming Chinese.

I immediately directed the cab driver to take me to the address I had been given for Kay Locke. She lived in an apartment on one of the upper floors of one of the tallest buildings in the city. Because I was so new and didn't know how to use the building's elevator, I carted my luggage up 15 or 20 flights of stairs. Exhausted, but grateful to have finally reached her apartment, I set my bags down on the floor beside her front door, rang the doorbell, and waited.

No one answered.

I rang again...still no answer. I kept on ringing, because I didn't know what else to do. I didn't have her phone number and had nowhere else to go. After about 20 minutes, the people in the next apartment cautiously opened their door to see what was going on. They spoke a little English; I spoke a little Cantonese; and between us I was able to communicate to them that I was looking for Kay Locke, the missionary.

"Oh, she is not home," they told me. "She is on furlough. She will not be back for six months."

Six months!

What was I going to do? I was in Hong Kong with little more than the clothes on my back, no way home, and Kay Locke was the only contact I had. She had had no advance knowledge that I was coming, so it was not her fault that she was not there when I arrived. Even so, it left me with a dilemma…what would I do now?

The late E. Thomas Brewster wrote two books, one entitled Bonding and the Missionary Task, and the other, Language Acquisition Made Practical: Field Methods for Language Learners, both of which emphasize the importance of missionaries on the field bonding quickly with the people they have come to serve. Becoming one with the people is one of the most critical factors for the success of any mission endeavor, especially on foreign soil or going into an alien culture.

Bonding is a very powerful force in nature, part of God's design for the welfare and survival of each new generation. It is a well-known fact, for example, that goslings will bond quickly with whatever creature they first meet immediately after hatching. If they are left with the mother goose, they naturally will bond with her. However, if they are removed from their mother shortly after hatching, and are cared for by a human, they will bond with that person as their "mother," and follow him or her. When a baby is born in the hospital, that child is placed with the mother as soon as possible, and for as long as possible, rather than being placed in the nursery, so that the newborn will bond with the mother rather than with the nursing staff.

In a similar vein, Brewster's books stress that missionaries entering the field in another nation should under no circumstances meet other people of their own nation, but immediately relate to the people they have come to serve. In fact, it is best to arrive early, on a date when no one is expecting you, when you are completely alone and basically helpless. And that is the best way to be. Why? Because if you are helpless, someone will eventually help you. If you are standing there, bewildered, surrounded by your luggage, and don't know what to do, either you will be forced to asked someone for help or someone will feel compelled to help you. Consequently, you will start to bond with those people.

In my case, the people who lived next door to Kay Locke invited me to stay with them. I did not actually lodge with them, but I did spend several hours with them. They even helped me find a place of my own that I could rent among the Chinese people, which was right where I needed and wanted to be. It would be many weeks before Kay would return from furlough, and in the meantime, I started to learn the language from the people. Furthermore, within two days I was eating with chopsticks. I was bonding with the people. It all seemed so natural. I never experienced any culture shock or had any problem adjusting to the Chinese people or their culture. I was becoming Chinese.

This was a different approach than that taken by many missionaries. In those days, most missionaries in a given region lived together in compounds with a few Chinese workers. Typically, a mission compound would be surrounded by a tall fence topped with barb wire, and with a guard dog added for extra security. Such a compound was a very intimidating place to visit, even for many Westerners, including myself. And the local people would never visit. So the only time missionaries would see or talk to any Chinese people were those few occasions each week when they left the compound to go to their churches in the city.

I did not have the opportunity or resources of a mission compound; I was on my own, humanly speaking. But I would not trade my experience for anything in the world, because I bonded with the Chinese people almost immediately, which significantly reduced the time it took me to earn their acceptance and trust.

Learning the language was a greater feat to accomplish. The United States Department of State has determined that Cantonese, the language spoken in Hong Kong, is one of the most difficult languages for Americans to learn, along with Japanese and Arabic. Cantonese is difficult for Americans because it is a tonal language—a very old language consisting of many different tones and many words for which there is no English equivalent. The tones are like pitches on a musical scale, where even the rising or falling of tonal inflection carries meaning. Mastery of this tonal aspect is absolutely essential for anyone who wishes to speak Cantonese well.

To give you an example, the Cantonese word for "five" is a nasal vocalization that can best be rendered in English as an "ng" sound. It took me two weeks to master that one sound alone. It is voiced through the nose, and there is nothing in the English language to compare it to.

Adding to the difficulty is the fact that this basic sound, along with many other sounds in Cantonese, can be "toned" or voiced seven different ways, and each way carries a different meaning. For Westerners or others trying to learn this language, this can produce some humorous or even embarrassing mistakes. For example, I remember someone who tried to say, "Our Father, who art in Heaven," but actually said, "Our pants are in the field." Another one tried to say, "I love the Chinese people; I want to get to know you," but it came out, "I like to butcher people; I want to eat you."

Difficulties of its tonal nature aside, the Chinese language includes no grammar or grammatical rules—no past, present, or future tense; no conjugation of verbs; no difference between singular and plural; and the same pronoun is used for he, she, and it. While it is possible to make Chinese grammatical, it is not necessary. The critical key to learning Chinese is to be among the people all the time...hearing it and speaking it...hearing it and speaking it, over and over again, day in and day out. But to speak it correctly, you must also receive a proper foundation in learning and distinguishing the proper tones, because the tones make all the difference.

In order to better learn the language, I was soon presented with an opportunity to attend New Asia College, which was a branch of the Chinese University. It was very expensive; at that time, tuition was 1,700 Hong Kong dollars for three months. Today, the cost is closer to 30,000 Hong Kong dollars. I attended for only three months, which cost 200 U.S. dollars, which is all the money I had or had been able to borrow.

My teacher, Janey Chen, who was a Christian, told me that the older missionaries had learned classic Chinese, which would be like present-day Americans learning Shakespearean English. Classic Chinese bears little resemblance to the Chinese actually spoken by the people, in a similar way to the fact that no one in the English-speaking world today speaks the English of Shakespeare. Furthermore, two lines of written classic Chinese might translate into many paragraphs as spoken by the people. Nevertheless, in 1911, as part of the revolution in China under Sun Yat-sen, the language was changed so that now the Chinese write and speak the same.

Janey recommended that I continue my language studies using a Chinese Bible as my textbook. She lived in a room of a large Chinese house that she rented from an older Chinese woman. With Janey's help, I was also able to rent a room in the same house. Consequently, Janey was often available to help me with any questions or problems I encountered with the language. This was a wonderful arrangement that I appreciated greatly; but actually, I did not have to call on her very often. I immediately started to study the Bible, and my text was the Gospel of John.

In the meantime, I was desperate to start a church. Sister Kiteley and all the good folks at Shiloh Church had paid my travel expenses to Hong Kong, and were also sending financial support every month. They believed that Jesus was returning soon and personally wanted to see the great end-time revival come. Thus, they were anxious for me to produce some results and did not really understand that it normally takes as long as three years to learn a new language. I felt some pressure from that end, but even more pressure was self-imposed. So I took a step of faith—I rented a room in May 1969, and told my landlady that I would be moving out in September to start a church.

But when September arrived, I could not find a place to move to, at any price. At that time, there was an extreme housing shortage in Hong Kong that was so severe that even rich people were forced to live in hotels. Nevertheless, through an ad in the newspaper, I finally found a place in Kowloon City, the Walled City made famous by the ministry of Jackie Pullinger to the drug addicts there. Yet when I went to look at the room, the owner apologized and stated, "I'm sorry, sir, but I cannot rent this room to you."

"Why not?" I asked. "Do you have something against foreigners?"

"Oh no, sir," she replied. "It's not that at all. It is only that this room has no window whatsoever. You deserve something better."

It was hot, and in those days they had no air conditioning. I assume she was probably worried that she would be held responsible if I suffocated or died of heat stroke, or something like that. So I continued to scour the newspaper ads for any suitable place to rent. I wasn't picky; I just wanted to be out among the people, and in a place where I could start a church.

By this time I had also become acquainted with a Chinese lady named Esther, who worked with Kay Locke in the drug addiction ministry. Esther also spoke English, and with her assistance, we located an advertisement listing a room for rent in an office building. Of course, in addition to a place to live, I was also looking for a place to start a church. When we called the landlord to inquire about the room, she asked what we wanted to use it for.

"I want to use it for a church," I replied.

"Praise the Lord!" she responded. "I'm a Christian. If you want to use the room for a church, I will reduce the rent."

At that time, the rent for the building was 600 Hong Kong dollars a month, which she reduced to 500. Under the rate of exchange that existed at that time, which was 5 to 1, this was the equivalent of 100 U.S. dollars a month, for a 500 square-foot space that could seat 40 to 50 people comfortably. And 100 U.S. dollars was the exact amount I was receiving each month from Shiloh. The space seemed perfect for what I wanted to do, but I had another problem—I still had no place to live.

When I informed the landlord of my situation, she said, "There is a large bathroom adjacent to the other room. Because you are single, it might be okay for you. Why don't you take a look at it?"

For a bathroom, it was large and long, but quite narrow; and only a simple partition had been constructed to separate the toilet area from the rest of the room. Nevertheless, I thought the room was perfect for my needs, which were few. Being adjacent to the room where

I would conduct the church services meant that I would not have to travel far between one and the other. I bought a little collapsible bed, obtained a small stove, and lived there for two years.

As a foreigner who wanted to immerse himself in a culture among 60,000 people, I thought this arrangement was perfect. And it wasn't long before I became somewhat of a local tourist attraction—many people came by to see this stranger living in such conditions. In their eyes, because I was an American, I had to be rich; yet most of them lived in larger places than I did. They could not understand why I would choose to live in such simple and austere circumstances.

Some of them, especially children, would say, "You must be very poor to live in such a small room."

"Well, really," I replied, "I have a very wealthy Father. He is the wealthiest person in the world. Do you know why I am living here?"

"Why?" they asked.

"Because I want to be your friend, and I want you to teach me Chinese."

Those children looked at me in amazement. "We be your teacher?" It was probably the first time that any adult had ever asked such a thing of them or suggested that they had anything worthy to offer.

"Yes," I replied. "I want you to be my teacher."

This was a wonderful arrangement for several reasons. First of all, children spoke perfect Chinese because it was their mother tongue, whereas the speech of adults was often influenced by various dialects from other parts of China. In addition, because they worked every day, adults had very little time to teach me; but children had several hours each day after school to spend with me. They were very patient, more so than most adults would have been. If I made a mistake, I could ask them 100 times how to say something, and they would patiently tell me over and over again. And they were free of charge! Best of all, my young tutors became the first children to attend the Sunday school of the church I was planting.

I'm sure a lot of people thought I was crazy, but I was saving money, getting to know the Chinese people, and developing precious relationships with these children and their families. Each time I came to a new word while reading the Gospel of John in Chinese, I would try to use it in a sentence. For instance, the Chinese word for "road" is tao ("the way"), from which we get "Taoism." I would go outside and ask someone, "What road (tao) is this?" And they would tell me. Once I had actually used a word, I tended to retain it easily. I also had a Chinese-English dictionary that I referred to whenever I needed.

After three months, I had read through the Gospel of John, and decided that it was time to start a church. At that time, I was teaching English Bible to a class of about 50 students in a small middle school. I told my students, "I am going to start a church. If you would like to come, you are quite welcome."

I had lived in Hong Kong for seven months by that time, and I was determined that from the very beginning I would not use an interpreter, but would do my own preaching in the Chinese language. Eight of my students came to the very first worship service, which I thought was amazing. In my simple Cantonese, which I'm sure contained many mistakes, I said to them, "This is the first time I have ever preached in Chinese. No doubt I will make mistakes, but I will do better. This is a new church. This is going to be a Spirit-filled church, and I believe that eventually it will be one of the largest churches in Hong Kong. We are going to bless China, because one day, China will open up."

After I finished preaching my simple message, I asked my students if any of them wanted to become a Christian, and they all said, "Yes." So in the very first meeting of my new church, eight people were saved! I was so excited! Although this success was on a much smaller scale, I imagined that this perhaps was how the Apostle Peter felt on the Day of Pentecost when he preached the Gospel and 3,000 people came to Christ. Not only was it the first time I had ever preached in Chinese, but it was also the first time that any of those eight students had ever been in church.

The first question my eight new converts asked after receiving Christ as their Savior and Lord was, "What do we do next?" I wanted to tell them about the baptism of the Holy Spirit, but I had not yet read the Book of Acts in Chinese, so I could not tell them about

Pentecost. The only Book of the Bible I had read was the Gospel of John. But I knew about prayer. So I encouraged all of them to go home and pray throughout the week.

When the following Sunday arrived, these eight new young Christians came back to church, and brought a few of their friends with them. One of the students, a young girl, was smiling and laughing, and began talking so fast that I could not follow her. Fortunately, Esther was there, and she translated for me.

"What is she saying, Esther?" I asked.

Esther replied, "She is saying, 'Last Sunday, you told us to go home and pray. Well, I was praying, and on Thursday I was hanging up clothes. All of a sudden, I just became so happy, and I began to speak in another language. I have been speaking in that language ever since, and it makes me feel that God is so wonderful! What is that? Why do I speak in this language?' "

I said, "That is what I want to tell you, but I do not have the vocabulary."

My lack of skill with the Chinese language at this early stage was no hindrance to the Holy Spirit, who brought Pentecost to these new believers in spite of my inability to teach it to them in their own language. Even in spite of my language inadequacies, our church was Spirit-filled from the very beginning.

CHAPTER NINE
INVADING THE DEVIL'S TERRITORY

Although much of my focus during my first seven months in Hong Kong was spent on immersing myself in the Chinese culture and learning the language, I also constantly thought about my call to preach the Gospel and minister to the Chinese people. It was against my nature to wait until I could speak fluent Chinese before beginning my ministry. Yet it was not just as simple as studying the language for a short while and then getting up one day and starting a church. It was very difficult at times, especially when I became involved in missions work by partnering with others who already had established ministries in the city. This brought me face-to-face with the realities of opposition, persecution, and deeply entrenched spiritual bondage and darkness.

As it turned out, the church I planted was located in the old part of Hong Kong, in an area known as the Western District. The people there, the Swatow, were old-fashioned, very traditional Chinese, which also means they were very superstitious and their lives steeped in idolatry.

My son-in-law, Samuel, who is now the senior pastor of our church, is from that area. He will be the first to tell you that evangelistic work among these old-style Chinese is incredibly difficult, because they are very extreme in whatever they do. As lost sinners who love the world, they completely give themselves over to the lusts, passions, and desires of the world. However, when they do come to Christ, they become very committed Christians. They love the Lord and give themselves over to Him as completely as they once gave themselves to the world. At first, the spiritual soil of their souls is fallow and hard and very difficult to break; yet once broken, that soil bears abundant fruit.

It is for this very reason that when I decided to plant a church among those people, many well-intentioned missionaries and other Christians in the city cautioned me that I would never succeed; it was too difficult an area, too steeped in superstition and spiritual darkness.

So what prompted me to start a church there, of all places, in spite of all the opposition? It all started when I got involved with a drug addiction ministry soon after my arrival in Hong Kong. I was working with Kay Locke as well as others who were involved in ministry to the drug addicts in the Walled City of Kowloon.

If there was any place on earth closest to hell, it would have been the Walled City, also known as Hak Nam, City of Darkness, particularly in the mid to late 20th century. Although it is gone now and replaced by a public park, the Walled City was at one time the most densely populated enclave in the world, with a peak population of as many as 35,000 people occupying a space only 6.5 acres in area. Like the rest of land-scarce Hong Kong, the only option for Hak Nam was to expand upward. It was a solid block of ramshackle buildings, separated at street level by dark and very narrow alleys, but interconnected at the upper levels by a series of stairs, ladders, and passageways. The buildings varied in height, with many as high as 14 stories, the highest they could be built without endangering aircraft arriving and departing from the nearby Kai Tak Airport. Otherwise, they probably would have been taller still.

Harkening back to its origin as a military fort in the 19th century, the Walled City received its name from the stone wall that originally enclosed the outpost. In 1842, in compliance with the terms of the Treaty of Nanjing, the Qing dynasty ceded Hong Kong Island to the

British. Hoping vainly to stem further British influence in the area, the dynasty made improvements to the small fort on the Kowloon Peninsula, including the construction of its defensive wall in 1847. When the New Territories were leased to Great Britain for 99 years in 1898, the Walled City was excluded. Nevertheless, the British attacked and seized the City the following year, and thereafter claimed ownership of it. But over the next four decades, they did very little with it. The City fell into decay, and in the 1930s, most of the crumbling structures were demolished. After the Japanese tore down the wall in 1940 to expand the nearby airport, the destruction of the City was virtually complete.

By 1945, the Japanese were gone, of course, and China announced its intention to reclaim its rights to the Walled City. Refugees by the hundreds swarmed into the area, and Hak Nam received a second lease on life. In 1948, the British tried and failed to expel the squatters, and thereafter essentially abandoned the City to its own devices. With no organized government oversight from either China or Great Britain, the Walled City quickly became a haven for drugs, prostitution, gambling, and crime of all kinds. Although many of the City's residents tried and succeeded in living a fairly normal life—working hard, making a living, and raising a family—even so, by the late 1950s the City was ruled by an organized crime syndicate known as the Triads. The Triads held sway for the next 20 years, until concerted efforts by the police, beginning in the mid-1970s and continuing for ten years, broke their power and influence and brought the crime rate under control.

But during the heyday of the Triads, crime was so rampant that the police would not enter except in large numbers. Even the tallest of the buildings were separated by alleys that were no more than six feet wide, and often even narrower. Open sewers ran down the alleys, and rats were everywhere, some of them larger than house cats. This was the state of the Walled City when I first arrived in Hong Kong, as it was for other missionaries who arrived before I did. Jackie Pullinger, who arrived in Hong Kong in 1966, is justly famous for her ministry to the drug addicts of Hak Nam, the story of which she recounts in the books, Chasing the Dragon and Crack in the Wall.

Drug users would put white powdered heroin on a piece of aluminum foil, heat it up with a match or a candle, and then inhale the fumes. Because of its resemblance to a dragon's tail, this practice became known as "chasing the dragon."

The Walled City was a very hard area—very difficult to penetrate with the Gospel. Nevertheless, I and others ventured into the City of Darkness many times to minister. Results generally were mixed. Many people we talked to were high from chasing the dragon. Most of the time they listened, but little else. It reminded me of the times I preached at the skid-row mission in California, where everybody was happy and friendly and appeared responsive on the outside, but few ever really got saved. Usually, the heroin fumes were so strong that we could not stay long in any one place; we'd start to feel like we were also getting high.

I have nothing but admiration for women like Jackie Pullinger, Kay Locke, and Donna Thorne, another pioneer missionary to this area of Hong Kong. There is so much controversy in the church today about the proper role of women in ministry. To be noted in this debate is the fact that in mission work around the world, it is usually women who do some of the most difficult and dangerous work. Their love for the Lord and heart for the lost impel them to go into places where most people would never dare venture, while teaching English or managing medical clinics. Jackie Pullinger took a job as a primary school teacher in the heart of the Walled City so that she could minister to the drug addicts and tell them about the love of Jesus. I estimate that in China, 60 percent or more of the preachers are women. While some people may not understand or appreciate it, the fact is that women often can open many more doors for the Gospel than can men. This is especially true in the case of Westerners trying to carry the message of the Gospel to the teeming masses of people in the cities, towns, and villages of the East. Because of the imperialism of the past on the part of Westerners toward China, many Chinese, particularly in the rural areas, are still very suspicious of Westerners, especially men. It is women who generally can make inroads with the people more easily.

Kay Locke and others who I worked with in drug addiction ministry during my first months in Hong Kong had rented space in a building in Kowloon City, just outside the Walled City, where they conducted church services and provided relief and other assistance to the people, particularly those trying to escape their addictions. Effective drug addiction ministry requires a place where addicts can go away from their normal environment, where they will not be confronted with the constant availability of drugs.

Our ministry had established a center for this very purpose on an island not far from the Western District. The idea was to provide a place where addicts could go into seclusion while they came off drugs and received job training, so they could reenter society as productive citizens. This was a great idea, in theory, but unfortunately did not work very well in practice. Somehow, drugs would always seem to follow and find their addicts, even those who were supposedly trying to kick the habit. Even at our facility on the island, with all its security and careful checks, dealers found ways to smuggle drugs inside. Drug addiction is a tough enemy that rarely surrenders without a long, hard, and bitter struggle. We dealt with cases where even drug addicts who became Christians continued to struggle with their addiction for months after being saved. Despite being in isolation on the island, they somehow still got their hands on drugs. Getting clean and sober and returning to society did not always mean that they were in the clear. All it would take was one moment of surrender, one moment of weakness, one cigarette, or one chasing-the-dragon, and their addiction would come roaring back. It was a very difficult problem.

I began working with this ministry soon after my arrival in Hong Kong, because I was so eager to get busy doing the Lord's work. I knew all along that I was to plant a church, but I also knew I could not ignore the tremendous spiritual need all around me, so I took every opportunity I could to preach the Gospel and share the love of Jesus. The drug addiction ministry was a meaningful outreach that helped many people come to Christ and find deliverance from their prison of dependency.

As it turned out, the dock where we boarded the boat to the island was very close to the location where I eventually planted my church in the Western District. One day I was on my way to the dock with Esther, who was working with us as a translator. As we rode the tram and passed through an area known as "Sai Ying Pun," which was actually part of the Western District, I turned to Esther, who lived in the area, and asked her if there were any churches there.

She looked at me with sadness in her eyes and said, "I am sorry to say that there are only two small churches in Sai Ying Pun. There is a small Baptist church with 30 or 40 people and an even smaller Lutheran church with 20 or 30 people. Both churches have been around for 30 or 40 years.

This information surprised me, because I knew that this area contained a population of about 60,000 people. "Why so few churches?" I asked. "And why are those two churches so small?"

Esther's next reply stunned me even more. "This is the devil's territory," she said. "These people do not want the Gospel. They are idol worshippers."

Sai Ying Pun was very close to the wharf where boats arrived from Communist China, and many of the people in the area were communists. They flew their red communist flags frequently. Especially on October 1, a Chinese national holiday commemorating the communist revolution in the country, red flags were displayed everywhere, and many of the people would sing songs of praise to Chairman Mao. They were communists and Buddhists at the same time—a very strange mix. On top of that, they also were very superstitious and very anti-Western. For these reasons, no missionary had ever succeeded in promoting Christianity.

Almost without exception during my three months of language school, every missionary told me that if I wanted to be successful in planting a church, I needed to go to a place called Kowloon Tong, which was in Kowloon City, near the old Kai Tak airport. The people there were well-educated and thoroughly westernized. It really was the easiest place to start another church or Christian school.

Well-intentioned as their counsel was, it never set well with me.

I had little interest in going into an area that was already Christian-ized. My passion—and my calling—was to take the Gospel into areas where it was not being preached and to people who had not yet heard of Christ. So when I heard Esther refer to Sai Ying Pun as "the devil's territory," I was moved very deeply in my spirit.

That is not right! I thought to myself. What does the Bible say? "The earth is the Lord's, and the fullness thereof." In fact, I actually began to get angry. How could you simply abandon 60,000 people to the devil?

"Many have tried," Esther assured me, "but no one has succeeded in preaching the Gospel there."

That was all I needed to hear. A sense of firm determination began to build up in me. "Lord," I prayed silently, "if You open the door, I will come here and start a church."

A few months later, as I related in the last chapter, I spoke with the landlord, who, as a Christian, was pleased to rent her building to me at a lower rate to use as a church. At that time I did not even know where the building was, so I asked her.

She replied, "It is in Sai Ying Pun."

The building I found was in the very area that Esther had called the devil's territory, and where I had promised to start a church if God would open the door! As far as I was concerned, this was clear and undeniable confirmation. Our words really do have power. I had confessed that, God willing, I was going to start a church in "the devil's territory," and God confirmed it. I was not going to surrender Sai Ying Pun to the devil.

It was not easy. I faced opposition every step of the way from many different quarters. First of all, I had arrived in Hong Kong with little more than the clothes on my back. Second, I knew very little Chinese, although I learned quickly thanks to the language school, and especially to the children who tutored me every day. I had almost no money and was living in a converted bathroom. For the most part, the people in the area where I sought to start the church were not very friendly, just as Esther had warned me. I had no coworker, but went out every day knocking on doors. Some people got mad and threw dirty water on me. Others cursed at me in Chinese. Time after time, people told me in no uncertain terms, "We are Chinese; we don't want your Western religion. We don't want your Western Jesus."

I did this day after day. For many days and across many months, I fasted and prayed, and all the time I kept knocking on doors and passing out tracts, sharing the message of Christ to anyone who would listen. It was hard work, but the Lord never promised it would be easy. Yet He did promise us strength and power for the journey. What He demands of us is faithfulness; and when we are faithful, He blesses.

As strong as the opposition was at first from the very people I was trying to reach, I faced an even greater opposition from many of the established churches and Christian ministries in the city. On the one hand, there were several churches that had begun well at one time, but over the years had degenerated into cults, with leaders who had fallen into deep error. Not surprisingly, these groups each claimed that they were the only true church, and that anyone who did not follow them was lost. On the other hand, there were the long-established Christian churches, solid in doctrine and theology, but nonetheless did not know of or believe in the baptism of the Holy Spirit. When I started my church in 1969, it was one of the few Spirit-filled churches in Hong Kong. I was committed to preaching the Gospel of Christ, yes; and I was also committed to teaching the baptism of the Holy Spirit, so I faced opposition on that front as well. For a long time, many of the established churches and pastors regarded me and my church as a cult.

Personally, being criticized for being charismatic never bothered me very much. The main problem I faced was that people from my church would occasionally go to other churches and hear all this criticism and become discouraged and sometimes confused. I "stuck to my guns," so to speak, regarding the baptism of the Holy Spirit, and we weathered the storm. Thankfully, those days are past. In fact, today there are more Spirit-filled churches in Hong Kong than there are churches that are not. But in the early days it was very difficult.

In those days, and particularly in the months before I started my own church, I frequently attended a church called New Life Temple.

Located in the Central District, not far from my own church in the Western District, New Life Temple was started in 1950 by Lester Sumrall as one result of a crusade held in Hong Kong by evangelist Morris Cerullo. Lester Sumrall, a great man of God who passed away a few years ago, gathered some wealthy businessmen together, purchased the building in the Central District, and started the church.

I attended the church primarily because it was one of the only Pentecostal churches around that actually preached the full Gospel. One day, sometime after I started my own church, I was speaking with Brother Sumrall. In the course of our conversation he asked me, "What are you doing these days, Mr. Balcombe?"

"I have started a little church," I replied. "We have a lot of students, and we're pretty busy with ministry."

Brother Sumrall shook his head. "You are just wasting your time," he said. "You need to reach the wealthy people. There is much money in Hong Kong. That is what I do. We have a meeting, get the wealthy people together, and they pay for everything. You are wasting your time trying to build a church with students. Students have very little money and cannot do very much."

I was rather upset over his remark because I was doing all I knew to do, and more importantly, I was seeing people get saved. Lester Sumrall was a great man of God, but God rest his soul, he and I disagreed on this point. The wealthy people he referred to, although not very spiritual, were appointed as elders and inevitably ended up controlling the church. In those days, many of Hong Kong's moneyed elite had obtained their wealth through corruption. That church still survives today, but has no more than 40 or 50 people, about the same as it had 50 years ago.

In contrast, I started my church with young people, and that approach has proven quite successful. I also focused on reaching the unsaved and building the church with them, rather than with seasoned Christians. I've discovered that the best age to focus on is 14 to 16 years. Students who are 17 or older focus and prepare extensively for the difficult government examination that they must pass in order to complete middle school, a British system that corresponds to high school in the United States. Following this exam is two years of matriculation, in which students prepare themselves to go on to college. It is a very different system from America, and highly competitive. Students preparing for that exam often have little extra time to devote to building a church and reaching out to people.

It was different with the younger students, however. For those students who were 14 to 16 years of age, the tests were still far enough away so as to pose little pressure on their minds and their time. They could come to almost every meeting at church, become very involved in what we were doing, and soon would be saved and filled with the Holy Spirit. Being Chinese, they already knew how to work and study hard. Now, as Christians, they also learned how to pray. As a result, they would get good test grades. As they grew older and continued to be involved in the church, they would grow in the Lord and grow in both character and integrity. Then when they entered the workforce, even at an ordinary or mundane job, they would quickly earn raises and promotions and eventually move into management because of their honesty and work ethic. Some would even eventually own the businesses they had originally worked for as employees.

This approach established a strong foundation for financial stability not only in the home, but also in the church. Consequently, even 40 years later and well into its second and third generations, our church is strong financially and is made up of hardworking and stable families. To my knowledge, there has not been a single divorce in our church in all these years, unless it involved people who came to us from another church. We have never had a church split, and today, counting all of our branches, we are one of the largest churches in Hong Kong. And it all began with young people.

Once the church was started, the Lord blessed us with growth that was steady, if not always fast. Even so, building the church was hard work, but the most satisfying work I had ever done. Then by 1971, two years after I had arrived in Hong Kong, I began to realize that a change was needed. The church was going well; people were being saved, healed, delivered, and baptized in the Holy Spirit. But something was missing. Slowly it dawned on me that I needed a partner in ministry—and not just a partner in ministry, but a partner in life. I needed a wife.

CHAPTER TEN

WHIRLWIND WEDDING

For a long time I had assumed I would never get married. From the day I was saved, gave my life to the Lord, and surrendered to His call, my focus had been single-minded—preach the Gospel and prepare to go to China. Marriage had never entered my mind as a serious option. Aside from the fact that I was very shy, socially awkward, and never had much interest in girls, I was also well aware of Paul's words to the Corinthians: "I would like you to be free from concern. An unmarried man is concerned about the Lord's affairs—how he can please the Lord. But a married man is concerned about the affairs of this world—how he can please his wife—and his interests are divided" (1 Cor. 7:32-34a NIV). I did not want to have divided interests. I did not want to be concerned about the affairs of the world, but only about the affairs of God. So with such a clear and focused call on my life, it seemed only logical that I would remain single.

Once I began pastoring my own church, however, I discovered it was not that easy, especially when the church consisted mainly of young people, including many young women. For an unmarried pastor, such a situation is fraught with potential difficulties and dangers. Moral temptation or misunderstanding can occur very easily, particularly in a one-on-one counseling situation. When I first started building my church in Hong Kong, I had no one helping me, no right-hand person by my side. The people I was most accountable to—the good people on staff of Shiloh Church, who had sent me to Hong Kong and who supported me regularly—were an ocean and half-a-world away. A single misstep by someone as young and inexperienced as I was could have been disastrous.

On the practical side, in addition to my work building the church, I had to cook my own food and wash and iron my own clothes. Having worked as a chef in a university dining hall, cooking was no problem. Laundry was another matter. I simply was not very good at it, particularly ironing. In those days, I wore a suit most of the time, so for speed and convenience I ironed only the front of my shirt. I did not know how to iron the back of it, but I didn't let that worry me, because it was covered up by my suit jacket.

In 1970, by the end of my second year in Hong Kong, I had come to the surprising conclusion that I needed to get married. It was more than just a practical decision; I believed that God had laid this awareness on my heart. Once that question was settled, I faced an even bigger question—Who? Who was I going to marry?

When word got around that I was looking for someone to marry, some people suggested that I marry one of the young women in the church. "No, that won't work," I told them. "As pastor of the church, I am the shepherd, and the shepherd is supposed to feed the flock, not eat the flock. If I married one of the young women in my church, it would be like eating one of my own sheep."

Even worse, if I chose one of the young women in the church to marry, I would run a great risk of stirring up jealousy and anger among the other young women, which would create division and unrest in the church. No, if I were to find a wife, I would have to go outside my church. I would have to go outside of Hong Kong. The only real choice I had, as I saw it, was to return to the United States.

That raised another problem. If I returned to the United States for an indefinite period, who would take care of my church? Who would care for the people I had reached for the Lord and who were just beginning to grow in their faith? I had no partner, no associate working with me, so if I went home to get married, my sheep would be without a shepherd.

Fortunately, a fellow pastor came to my rescue. Elijah Chan, a Spirit-filled man from an evangelical background, offered to help me out. "Dennis," he said, "I will take over your church for you while you are gone. I will come and preach every Sunday. But you have to be back in three months, because that is all the time I can give. I cannot stay any longer."

That was certainly better than nothing. I knew that without a pastor, my church would be finished in only two or three weeks. I had worked too hard and too long, and the Lord had blessed too much, for me to allow it to fall apart. I trusted Pastor Chan and knew that my people would be well cared for. I had to travel to California, get married, and return to Hong Kong in three months. That was all there was to it.

It wasn't as though I had absolutely no idea who I might marry. During the entire two years I had been in Hong Kong, I had received regular letters of encouragement and support from numerous members of Shiloh Church in San Francisco. At the time I had left to come to Hong Kong, Pastor Violet Kiteley had encouraged the congregation to write to me on a regular basis. She knew that this moral support would be just as important to me as financial support would be, and she was absolutely right.

I enjoyed and drew comfort and encouragement from all the letters I received, but it was not long before the correspondence from one particular person began to stand out. Twice a month, almost without fail, I received sensitive, insightful, and encouraging letters from a young woman I had never met personally, but who had begun attending Shiloh Church about four months before I had left. Her name was Kathy Bissell.

One reason Kathy's letters struck such a responsive chord in me was because she was no stranger to mission work. The daughter of Presbyterian medical missionaries, Kathy was born in 1950 in Chiang Mai, Thailand. She and her siblings grew up speaking Thai, even before they could speak English. Her parents worked at the Presbyterian Hospital in Chiang Mai, where her father, a medical doctor, supervised all other physicians, and her mother ran the nursing school. A few years after Kathy's birth, her family moved to Prae, a much smaller village in Thailand, where her father worked at the village hospital, a much smaller facility.

In 1958, when she was eight years old, Kathy's family returned to the United States on furlough. What normally would have been a one-year stay in the United States was extended when her father decided to go back to school to become a specialist in internal medicine. Their one-year furlough turned into a five-year extended stay. By the time they were ready to return to the mission field, the mission society that had appointed them had decided that their medical skills were needed in India more than in Thailand. So in 1963, just as Kathy was ready to enter the seventh grade, she and her family moved to India. There she experienced for the first time the common existence of countless missionary children overseas—boarding school. While their parents labored in an area blighted by extreme and blatant poverty, Kathy and her two older brothers lived and studied at an American boarding school located in a beautiful mountain resort area of India, three days and nights by train from their parents. Her younger sister was only four at the time and attended a school on the mission compound where her parents lived.

The Bissells' five-year tour in India was cut short in 1966 when Kathy's father suffered a serious nervous breakdown because of the constant pressure of his work and environment. Kathy was in boarding school at the time. Her two older brothers had already graduated and returned to the United States to attend college. The rest of her family were to return to the United States on emergency leave so that her father could receive treatment. When Kathy's mother asked her to go along, Kathy declined, saying she wanted to first finish out her junior year of high school. Her family went stateside, while she remained in India. Five or six months later, upon finishing her school year, Kathy traveled halfway around the world by herself, at age 16, and was reunited with her family in California.

Kathy testifies that this was a very dark and sad time in the life of her family. Her father was very sick, and for a time was even committed to a mental institution. But God turned even this sorrowful time to His glory, because it was during the months following their return to the United States that most of Kathy's family received the baptism of the Holy Spirit and came to know Christ in a new and powerful and joyous way. It began with one of her brothers, and then her mother received the baptism. Kathy remembers getting off the airplane in California to be greeted by her mother, who displayed a joy and peace Kathy had never seen in her before, and which seemed all the more remarkable in light of her father's illness. Kathy told her mother, "I want what you have," and before long, Kathy, too, received the baptism of the Holy Spirit. Eventually, even Kathy's father was baptized in the Holy Spirit, and the entire family began attending a Spirit-filled church. He even went back to work at Kaiser Hospital in the Los Angeles area, where he remained until he retired.

Kathy attended her senior year of high school in California, and when she graduated at the age of 18, enrolled in the University of San Francisco nursing school, which was run by the Jesuits. Although she lived in the dormitory during the week, on weekends she stayed with her brother, Keith, and his wife, Linda, who were attending Shiloh Church in Oakland. Kathy began attending with them, which is where she first learned of me, only four months before I left for Hong Kong.

By the time Kathy began attending Shiloh Church, she had already experienced two significant events in her life that made it easy for us to connect both emotionally and spiritually. First of all, she had experienced the baptism of the Holy Spirit and knew His power firsthand, because He transformed her life completely. The Holy Spirit filled her with a joy like she had never known before and changed her from a shy person who had trouble making friends into an outgoing person deeply in love with Jesus. The baptism and power of the Holy Spirit are central to my message and ministry, and Kathy understood this from the start and was in full agreement. Second, Kathy had already felt God's call to return to Asia as a missionary. Even though we did not meet for the first time until we were both young adults, God had been preparing Kathy over the years for our ministry together, just as

He had been preparing me.

Of course, neither of us realized all of this immediately. Our correspondence back and forth began shortly after my arrival in Hong Kong, and continued for two years until 1971, when I came back to the United States for the purpose of getting married. The reason Kathy began writing to me was not because she was interested in me personally, at least not at first. She had heard me speak about my call and passion for China, and because of her background as a member of a missionary family, as well as her personal call to missions, she took great interest in what I had to say. After I left for Hong Kong, Pastor Violet Kiteley encouraged church members to commit to write to me at least once a month, and Kathy accepted the challenge. She understood from personal experience how uplifting letters of support and encouragement can be for persons serving on a foreign field.

For the first year or so, my responses to Kathy's letters took the form of writing a brief personal note to her at the bottom of the mimeographed church newsletter I mailed every month. I wrote polite things like, "Thank you for your letters—they really encourage me." At that time I did not even really know who she was. I was familiar with her name but had never met her. But there was something in her letters. Her spirit and her insights soon began to resonate with me. She had a way of saying just what I needed to hear at just the right time. Gradually, I began to write her more and more—no longer just a polite statement at the bottom of the newsletter—and my letters to her took on an increasingly personal tone. At one point, I asked someone I knew from the church who was also writing me, if he could get a picture of Kathy and send it to me. Despite our developing relationship through letters, I was still too shy to ask her directly.

By the time I arrived in California in January 1971, Kathy was figuring pretty strongly in my mind as the most likely candidate for my wife, even if I did not fully realize or acknowledge it at that time. From my point of view, things looked pretty promising, but the increasingly personal nature of my letters to her almost scared her off. At this point, I think it would be best to let Kathy tell the story in her own words.

During the few months immediately before Dennis came stateside in January 1971, his letters to me became very personal in tone. He confided to me statements like, "I have been praying for a wife;" "I know God is preparing a wife for me;" and "When I come back I would really like to see you. I would really like to get to know you." One time he even went as far as to say, "I think you might be the one!" In this regard, Dennis was like the Apostle Paul, who confessed to the Corinthians that he was "timid when face-to-face with you, but bold when away" (2 Cor. 10:1b NIV).

I said to myself, Whoa! Wait a minute! This is getting heavy. I really need to pray about this. Is this really God? I know I have a missionary call, but do I want to follow this man back to the mission field? Do I really love him? I don't even know him.

When Dennis came to church for the first time after arriving in the States, he was the man of the hour. Everyone crowded around him after the service. After all, he was "their missionary." Many of the young women regarded him as the catch of the year, if not the century! I know of several girls who had a crush on Dennis. As for me, I just wanted the chance to meet him face-to-face and talk to him, but I found it hard to approach him because he was constantly surrounded by other people all the time. Finally, one day I persisted and managed to get close to him and say, "Hi, Dennis. I'm Kathy, the one you've been writing to."

He looked at me, and his face turned beet red. Despite the boldness in his most recent letters to me, he was very shy toward me in person. He smiled, though, and managed to say, "Oh, hello. Nice to meet you." He was so nervous that he suddenly looked like he wished he were anyplace else but there.

Dennis had told me in some of his letters that we needed to go out and talk together when he arrived stateside, and I gave him plenty of opportunities to ask. When he spoke about his work in China at several different services, I was always there, hoping and expecting that at some point he would ask me out. But after sticking around for a few minutes to talk to people, he would simply leave. It almost seemed as though he was ignoring me. I would think, Well, fine...

whatever....

Before long, people began inviting Dennis for dinner, and eventually his boldness came to the fore. After receiving one particular invitation, he asked, "Can I bring Kathy with me?"

They said that was fine, so Dennis asked me to accompany him. Then I started going with him on a regular basis. I think he felt safer at that time being with me in the presence of others rather than being alone with me. During dinner, the conversation naturally turned to Hong Kong, and the hosts would ask Dennis when he was going back. The first time he was asked this, his answer shocked me. Instead of saying, "When I go back...," he said, "When we go back...." It was like he had already made his mind up that I was going to marry him and go back to Hong Kong with him. The only problem was that he had not even proposed to me yet. Dennis was a man of faith and very focused, even then. He knew God would prepare the right one, and he just spoke it out by faith.

On my part, I just prayed about it. It wasn't like I fell madly in love with him at first sight or anything like that. I kept praying about it, asking, "God, is Dennis the right one? Is he the one You have prepared for me? I know You have called me to be a missionary. Is it Your will that I fulfill that call by marrying Dennis and joining him in his work in Hong Kong?" Eventually, God gave me a peace about it, and I became convinced that Dennis was the right one, and that he was going to be my husband.

One of the things Dennis liked to do was drive up in the hills around the Oakland area. Often, he and I would go on long drives after the service and talk. One night he said, "Let's go for a drive." We got into the car and took off. For a long while, he drove and drove without saying a word. I kept looking at him, expecting him to start the conversation, but he remained silent. I then began to wonder if he was angry with me.

Finally, after about an hour, he drove back to our apartment building where he and I both had apartments. He parked the car in front of the building, looked at me, and said, "All night I have been trying to find the boldness to ask you a question, and I have not been able

126

to. That is why I haven't said anything. But I have to tell you—I love you, and I want to marry you."

It was as simple as that. No flowers, no ring, no romantic candle-light dinner. Straight and to the point—that was Dennis's way.

"Dennis," I said, not quite sure how to respond, "it's one o'clock in the morning, and I'm tired. Can I give you an answer tomorrow?"

"No, no, no," he replied. "Let's get out of the car. Why don't we go up to my apartment and talk about this?"

So we went up to his apartment. I sat down and he sat down next to me. He said to me again, "Really, I love you and I want to marry you. Please say yes. Give me an answer tonight. Otherwise I won't let you go."

I was sitting there thinking, Okay, I have been praying about this, so now the time has come. I looked at Dennis and said, "Yes, I will marry you."

Dennis was ecstatic. He pulled out a calendar and said, "When are we going to get married? What day?" It was like he was in a big hurry, like he had to get back to Hong Kong right away.

Any other girl probably would have hit him on the head and said, "Forget it!" But there I was, considering him, with a calendar in his hand. Then he asked, "How about two weeks from now?"

Then I looked at him as though he had lost his mind. "What? Two weeks? Are you crazy? I can't get a wedding together in two weeks!"

Dennis looked at his calendar again. "What about April the third?" That was his birthday. "Why don't we get married on April the third? That is a good day and it is about four weeks away. That will give you plenty of time."

Maybe I was the one who was crazy now, because I said, "Okay."

I went into my apartment and was so tired that I went straight to bed. I was so quiet that I did not even disturb the female friend who was staying with me that weekend. She was sound asleep, and I quickly joined her. When I woke up the next morning, she was already up and getting dressed. Then the memory of the previous night flooded over me.

"Oh, Kris," I said, "what have I done?"

She looked at me with concern in her eyes. "What happened?"

"Last night I told Dennis I would marry him!"

Kris started laughing. "That's the funniest thing I've heard in a long time!"

"Oh no," I said. "It's true. Dennis asked me to marry him, and I told him yes."

When Kris realized I was telling the truth, she got very excited. "Wow! That's great! Praise God!"

All day I walked around in shock. I had agreed to marry a man I hardly knew, and we were getting married in four weeks!

I called my mom and said, "Mom, I have some news for you. Are you sitting down? I'm getting married!"

She just said, "That's nice, dear. To whom?" She didn't sound worried or bothered at all.

I said, "Well, have you heard about Dennis Balcombe, that missionary to China?"

"Yes," Mom replied, "I have heard about him. I thought that maybe the two of you would get together." It was like she had some sort of intuition or word of knowledge.

"But Mom," I said, "here's the kicker—we are getting married in four weeks."

That's when my mom lost her calm demeanor. "What?" she gasped. "Four weeks!" If she wasn't sitting down before, she was now.

And when Dennis's family found out, they were almost as ecstatic as he was.

The next four weeks were a whirlwind. It was like Hurricane Kathy had hit the California coast as I scrambled to get ready for the big event. Fortunately, I had a lot of help. After her initial shock, my mom was very enthusiastic, as was the rest of my family. Sometimes it was tough, but I was committed. I was not going to back out. I had told Dennis yes, and I was going to follow through. Besides, I knew in my heart that it was the right thing to do. I knew Dennis loved me, and I loved him. At the same time, I was trying to get to know him. There were times in the midst of it all when the reality of the situation would hit particularly hard, and I would think, I'm about to marry a man I hardly know except through letters. I'm going to cross the ocean with him to the other side of the world, and who knows when, if ever, we will be back. What am I doing? Am I crazy? Everyone else was saying, "Oh, it's so wonderful!" while I was agonizing, Oh, what am I doing? If I had not had the Lord on my side helping me, I don't think I would have gone through with it. I would have called the whole thing off and just said, "I'm sorry. Good-bye."

But…

Our wedding was absolutely beautiful. The entire occasion was an absolute miracle. There were four bridesmaids, and 500 people in attendance; and afterward, we had a sit-down sandwich with afternoon tea. It was amazing how the people of Shiloh really supported me. My family supported me, and my parents were totally behind me. It was truly remarkable.

At the wedding, I walked down the aisle to the music of the traditional "Bridal March." Some people had joked about playing "Happy Birthday" because it was Dennis's birthday, but they didn't (thank goodness)! My father gave me away, and as I faced Dennis in front of all those witnesses and well-wishers, I calmly sang to him, "Whither thou goest, I will go. Whither thou lodgest, I will lodge. Your people will be my people."

Everyone in the room was touched by the song, and some even were weeping, because they knew that Dennis had pledged to live and die in China. In fact, when he first left for Hong Kong, and thoughts of marriage had not even entered his head, he told everyone that he probably was not coming back. He had a one-way ticket to Hong Kong, and that was all he needed. So when I sang that song at our wedding, everyone knew that I was committing my life not only to Dennis, but also to China. We had no idea when, or if, we would return. The important thing was that we were together, obedient to God's call, and we knew He would take care of us.

The wedding service itself lasted a couple of hours because we had a time of worship, a time of prophetic word, and a time of preaching. We almost had an altar call. It was during our wedding ceremony that one of Dennis's brothers, Doug, was so touched by the Holy Spirit that he surrendered his life to the Lord and answered the call to become a minister of the Gospel.

Following our whirlwind wedding, Dennis and I embarked on a wild honeymoon. Well, maybe not wild, but certainly unusual, because Dennis preached everywhere we went. We drove the entire West Coast, as far south as Tijuana, Mexico and as far north as Vancouver, British Columbia, preaching in church services in town after town. We even spent a few days in Lake Tahoe.

Along the way we experienced a couple of mishaps. I became sick from something I ate in Tijuana, and we had to stop at every gas station along the way. Then one time our car broke down, and on another occasion, someone broke into our car and stole all the monetary gifts we had received at the wedding. All in all, however, it was a wonderful time.

Right after our honeymoon, we flew to Hong Kong. We were married on April 3, 1971, and arrived in Hong Kong in May to begin our life together. Dennis's church of a few dozen people was now my church. His call to China was now my call. "Whither thou goest, I will go. Whither thou lodgest, I will lodge. Your people will be my people."

And so it was.

CHAPTER ELEVEN
SHOCKWAVES

To present a unique and distinctive perspective to the story of our earliest years together, Kathy will speak again in this chapter. When we arrived together in Hong Kong in May 1971, the city had already been home to me for two years. I was fluent in Cantonese, and had planted a church that was slowly but steadily growing. Whereas, even though Kathy had spent her childhood and adolescent years on the mission field, she still was entering a world completely foreign to her, both culturally and socially.

I must confess that because of my familiarity with Hong Kong, and my single-minded focus on the ministry to which the Lord had called me, and due to certain aspects of my own personality, I was not as sensitive as I should have been to the enormous challenges that Kathy faced. Not only did she have a whole new culture and language to learn, but she had just married a man she barely knew. Her confidence that all of this was according to God's will did not necessarily make her adjustments to these changes any easier. But we both attest to the fact that God gave her the grace not only to put up with me (no small challenge, at times), but also to fully adapt to and embrace her new world.

What was it like for Kathy in those early days? I'll let her tell you.

When I first arrived in Hong Kong with Dennis, everything was a shock—the people, the language, the city itself. I had spent most of my growing-up years in Thailand and India, and most of that time in small villages and rural areas. I was not accustomed to large cities, particularly one as large as Hong Kong, with its population of four million (at that time). Even though I found myself quickly drawn in by the culture and vibrancy of the city, the challenges I faced, particularly during the first year, were so daunting that even today, I regard it as miraculous that I survived without throwing up my hands and retreating back to California.

We had barely gotten settled in when Dennis said, "Kathy, the first thing you need to do is learn the language. I want Janey Chen to teach you. She is the one who taught me, and I think she is the best."

That sounded fine to me. I was eager to learn the language and become acquainted with the people of Hong Kong. Then Dennis dropped his bombshell.

"There is something else I need to tell you," he continued. "From now on, I am not going to talk to you in English; I am going to talk to you in Chinese only. That way you will be able to learn the language faster."

I know Dennis meant well. After all, that was the way he became fluent in Cantonese so quickly—by immersing himself in the language, like a non-swimmer plunging into the deep end of a swimming pool and swimming to the side because he has to. I listened as he talked, but had little reaction at first. Everything was coming at me so quickly that I didn't have a chance really to think about it at the time. However, after a couple days of hearing nothing but Chinese coming out of the mouth of my new husband, I realized that this was not going to cut it.

"This is not going to work," I informed Dennis. "I'm not saying that I'm not going to learn Chinese; this is about you not speaking to me in English anymore. You are my husband. I love you and I want to communicate with you…but I can't. I could leave you, not on the grounds of lack of communication, but on the grounds of zero communication. I would really, really like to talk to you."

Fortunately, Dennis recanted and started speaking to me in

English again. "Okay," he said, "I will give you a year to learn the language. After that, I will talk to you only in Chinese."

That sounded reasonable to me. After all, I was studying the language full-time and was immersed in it on a daily basis. I heard it everywhere I went, and quickly discovered that the practical necessity of conversing in a language greatly enhances the learning process. It truly is the best way to learn a language.

So, during one of my first days in Hong Kong, Dennis took me to the market. As we walked by the various stalls, he pointed out the different items of produce and called them by their Chinese names. It was a "wet" market, where the chickens were alive and the fish were swimming. After we finished, Dennis said, "Okay, tomorrow you can do this for yourself."

At my look of surprise, Dennis explained, "You are the wife. In Chinese culture it is the wife who goes to market and buys food for the day."

To my relief, I discovered that this was not nearly as hard as I expected it to be. In fact, after that one trip with Dennis, I was able to shop successfully at the market by myself. It was not like shopping in the modern supermarkets of the day, where you grab a shopping cart, choose your items, take them to the cashier, and pay with a credit card. The wet market is a noisy place, where everything is alive and produce is stacked everywhere. Prices are posted in Chinese, and price haggling or bargaining is expected.

In addition to the challenge of learning a difficult language, I also did not yet know the monetary units used in Hong Kong. But I quickly learned. Even if I could not call something by its name, I could always point, and the people were always very nice and understanding, and helped me learn each Chinese name and the cost of each item. Truly, there is no better incentive to learning a language than being in a situation where you are forced to use it on the fly.

After only six months or so, I had gotten to the place where I could understand most of what people were saying, and generally could speak well enough for them to understand me. At the same time, in my language studies, Janey Chen had taken me directly to the

Scripture, teaching me Bible words and terms in Chinese, which she explained was vital for me to learn as a missionary. Six months later, even as I was learning to make my way with the Chinese language in day-to-day social settings, I also learned how to give a simple testimony for Christ. The first time I shared it in public, I read every word from a written copy, and was shaking the whole time, but I accomplished it. Within a year, I was fluent enough to talk to someone without completely blowing it and embarrassing myself.

With regard to our church life, I had come into a congregation that had already been established and functioning. The small group was accustomed to Dennis as their "Papa," their pastor, and now I had entered the picture. It was a little awkward at first. I'm not saying that they did not accept me; they did…with much love. However, adjustment was necessary on both sides.

It greatly helped matters that I chose to quickly take over everything a pastor's wife is "supposed" to do. There was no Sunday School in the church when I arrived; so, it became my job to start one. I also led worship and the choir. All these activities afforded me high visibility with the congregation, and helped me interact with them in many different ways, which made the adjustment period easier for everyone.

Dennis was aware that I could play the piano, so one day he plopped the hymn book in front of me and said, "We are going to sing these songs on Sunday. I would like you to play them."

I looked at him in horror. "I don't know how to play these!"

With a puzzled look he responded, "But you told me you could play the piano."

"I can play Mozart, Beethoven, and that sort of thing. But hymns are completely different." I had been trained in classical piano and had performed in concerts at school with the other students. I was confident playing classical piano pieces, but put a hymn in front of me, and it was like, "What do I do now?"

Dennis looked disappointed, so I quickly added, "Okay, I'm willing to learn. Just give me the songs a week in advance, and I will learn them." This arrangement worked fine—except for those times when Dennis would suddenly get an inspiration for another song and throw it at me at the last minute. I did my best, and all in all, I adapted to church life relatively quickly.

I wanted to support Dennis and be a suitable help to him in this ministry. I worked hard to learn to play those hymns, and it became easier as time went on. Although I had never led a choir before, I had sung in a choir all my life and had learned a fair amount of knowledge during those years, so leading was not that difficult. Likewise, teaching Sunday School was no problem for me. I loved children and enjoyed telling Bible stories using a flannel graph and cutout figures.

While adapting to church life was challenging at times, adapting to married life was even more so. When Dennis and I got married, I hardly knew him, and he barely knew me. Our marriage went completely against the conventional wisdom that says a couple needs to spend time to get to know each other before getting married. For us, getting to know one another was the main preoccupation of the early months of our marriage. By most human standards it was not the wisest or healthiest way to start a lifelong relationship. Had I not received a revelation from God that our marriage was ordained by Him, I never would have gone through with it. Even at the time, some people thought I was crazy. "What are you doing? What are you thinking?" I did not fully understand what God had in mind; I just knew that marrying Dennis was what He wanted me to do. Dennis felt the same way. We both sensed that God was leading us to this union, and we trusted Him to help us work everything out.

Dennis is in many ways a very complicated and different type of person. He is one of the most focused people I have ever known. He possesses a devotion to ministry and to China that is laser-like in its intensity, which I realized before we were married. It is one of the many reasons why I love him, and I honor him for it. At the same time, his single-minded focus sometimes made things difficult for me because I had to learn how to understand and appreciate his view and become part of his life plan. This is not to say that he did not love me; he did. But he was learning too. Being married was just as new an experience for him as it was for me. In many ways, I was as much a stranger to him as he was to me, and he was, in his own way, struggling to adjust just as much as I was.

Another characteristic I love about Dennis is that he is a very transparent and honest person. He is a perfect example of "what you see is what you get." I have never been surprised to learn something about him of which I had not known before. He has never hidden anything from me. I knew before we married that Dennis's call to China was an all-consuming call on his life. He was quite upfront about that. He had spent two years working tirelessly, knocking on doors, sharing the love of Jesus, and building a church from scratch in one of the most difficult areas of Hong Kong. The challenge we both faced in the early days of our marriage was how to adjust to make me a full partner with him in his ministry, so that we could grow and build and fulfill this great calling together.

During those first few months after we arrived in Hong Kong, I spent most of my time getting to know my husband. It was actually a mutual project—I was discovering his strengths as well as his faults, and he was discovering mine. Sometimes it was embarrassing, sometimes frustrating, sometimes comical, but always enlightening! The most positive result that came out of all of this, aside from growing closer and more deeply in love with the man I married, was that I learned how to find fulfillment for all my desires in the Lord. I loved Dennis, and I knew he loved me; but I discovered very early on that no human being, no matter how perfect, can ever meet all my needs. Every couple has expectations when they marry: He is going to complete me and make me whole; she is all I'll ever need...that sort of thing. But those expectations can never be met by another person, at least not fully; and that can lead to disappointment, anger, and conflict. Dennis was not "Mr. Perfect," nor was I "Mrs. Perfect." We were two imperfect people who had to learn how to get along, build a home and family together, and fulfill a divine calling...and by the grace of God, we did.

The magnitude of the challenges and life changes that I faced during those early months drove me to the feet of Jesus in total surrender, and it was there that I found my completeness. Did I ever want to give up? Did I ever feel like throwing in the towel and leaving? Yes. There were times when I wanted to say, "I'm out of here. Bye!" But the Lord always gripped my heart and pulled me back. He promised with words of comfort, "I am your satisfaction. I am your desire. I am your source for everything you could ever need or want. If you will release everything in your life to Me, place every burden on My shoulders, I will bless you with a healthy, strong, and fruitful marriage." I did—and He did. Everything worked out for good. It wasn't always easy; it wasn't as though I never had any emotional difficulties, or that I never cried. In fact, I cried a lot. I had many questions about many things, but I always found God right there with me, ready to carry me through. That is where my relationship with the Lord became exclusively the two of us.

As I adjusted to my new life, I really wanted to help out in the day-to-day work of building the church, of getting out among the people and talking to them. In this respect, a young Chinese woman named Esther was a true blessing from God to me. Esther was the secretary for the church, and although she was Chinese, she spoke perfect English. A few years older than me, she had a very loving, caring, and compassionate spirit, and she quickly took me under her wing. Many were the times that Esther and I went out knocking on doors, passing out tracts, visiting people, and inviting them to church. Because I was still learning the language, Esther took the lead in these contacts. I learned so much just by watching her and listening to her, and my facility with the Chinese language grew much more quickly as a result.

I also found in Esther a woman in whom I could confide regarding many of my struggles and questions in those early months. I did not tell her everything I was going through—some matters were just too personal—but I came to highly value her wise counsel and appreciated her empathy on the matters I did share with her. Esther was quick to give me hugs and was always ready to pray with me, and that meant so much to me. She was a true friend, and remains so today, even though she now lives in California.

There were many times when I also went out with Dennis to visit the people. Normally, this was a very enjoyable experience for me, except for those times when Dennis forgot to translate for me. I was still learning the language, and I would stand there, trying desperately to follow along as Dennis and the person he was talking to rattled off rapid-fire Chinese. It was as though Dennis became so engrossed in the conversation that he momentarily forgot I was with him, or at least forgot that I could not understand or speak the language nearly as well as he could. Every now and then I would nudge him in the side and ask, "What did they say?" This was another type of situation that motivated me to become fluent in Chinese as quickly as possible.

Another confidant I had in those early days who was a real lifeline to me was my mother. I called Mom a lot, and even today I thank God that she was always there. I felt like I could share anything with her. I unburdened my heart and poured out my questions, my uncertainties, my frustrations with Dennis, and the difficulties I was having simply trying to adjust. Mom was always sympathetic and completely nonjudgmental. She never took sides or expressed empty sentiment. She never said things like, "Oh, that horrible husband of yours," or "You poor thing." Instead, she would say, "I understand, dear, and I am praying for you." Then she would give me some really great advice that helped me see things from a different perspective.

Many of our conversations focused on my struggles and frustrations while getting to know Dennis and learning how to relate to him. Mom generally listened while I did most of the talking, and when I was done she would say, "God knows everything, so take everything to Him. Remain steadfast. Think on all the positive things you know about Dennis. Think on the good things that you saw in him and why you married him. Work on those things, and then, when you have a chance, talk with him."

Early on, I often found it very difficult to talk to Dennis about certain things, particularly when I was frustrated with him or felt that he was insensitive to my feelings or needs. And every now and then, when I got bold enough or frustrated enough, I would raise these issues with him. Sometimes he would agree and say, "I'm sorry. I will do my best to be more sensitive in the future." At other times, after praying through the issue, I would discover that it was me, not Dennis, who needed to change. It was me who needed the attitude adjustment, and sometimes I found it necessary to apologize to him.

The issues that Dennis and I faced in the early months of our marriage were no different, essentially, from those that most married couples have to deal with. We had to get to know each other just as other couples do, but that process was made even more challenging because I was trying at the same time to learn a new language and adjust to life in a different culture. But part of the process was what every couple experiences—simply recognizing the different ways that men and women think and approach problems.

Sometimes, when sharing my troubles with Dennis, all I really wanted was a sympathetic, listening ear, and someone to pray with me. Yet many times, Dennis would listen for about five minutes and then say, "Oh, I know what your problem is," and then go on for half an hour, telling me how to solve it.

One time when he responded this way, I listened until he was finished, and then said, "Dennis, would you please pray with me? That's all I want you to do."

He arched his eyebrows in surprise. "Really? That's all you want?" He seemed genuinely shocked that what I wanted was not an explanation or a solution, but a listening ear and a prayer partner.

Truth is, we both had a lot to learn in the relationship department. As time went on, I got better about sharing, Dennis got better at listening, and we both got better at understanding each other.

Another situation I had to get used to was waking up in the middle of the night to find Dennis gone. Dennis normally sleeps no more than three to four hours a night. He goes to bed late and rises early, and spends most of those early hours in prayer. When I would wake up in the wee hours of the morning and find myself alone, I had to trust that my husband was either at church praying, or praying on one of the long walks he loved to take.

Dennis has always loved to take walks. In those early years, he became familiar with the hills of Hong Kong, even places that most residents of Hong Kong had never been to. He would drive up into the hills, park the vehicle, and start to hike. One time while he is was out roaming, he fell into a dry well. Fortunately, the well was not deep and he was able to climb out. If it had been too deep, he probably would have died there and no one would have ever known what had happened to him. I would not have had the faintest idea where to start looking for him and would have been forced to report a missing person. And it is highly unlikely that searchers would have thought to look for him in an empty well. Fortunately, Dennis arrived home later that morning, scratched up and muddy, but otherwise all right.

After only a matter of months, we faced the first real crisis of our young marriage. I became pregnant. However, the fertilized egg never descended all the way into the uterus but remained caught in the fallopian tube, resulting in an ectopic pregnancy. This type of pregnancy is very dangerous. As the fetus grows, it causes the fallopian tube to burst, and the mother can bleed to death. In many cases, the only symptom that these women experience is some pain; consequently, they do not even know they are pregnant.

Likewise, I had no idea I was pregnant. I was experiencing pain, but did not know the cause. Furthermore, I did not go to a doctor, because I did not know any doctors in Hong Kong. This was a different experience for me. While growing up, I had always lived with a doctor and a nurse in my own home—my parents.

My only symptoms were pain in my right side and a general sense of not feeling well.

Then one morning, with no warning, I suddenly fainted—boom. Everything went black. Fortunately, Dennis was home at the time. That in itself was a minor miracle, because he was so often gone at that time of the day. If he had been away when I passed out, he would have come home to find that I had already gone to Heaven. But by the grace of God, Dennis was there and saw me keel over.

He immediately called a good friend and coworker of ours, Pastor Chen. And in almost a panic, Dennis blurted out, "My wife has just fainted! What do I do?"

Without any hesitation, Pastor Chen responded, "I am coming over immediately in a taxi, and we will take her to the hospital."

When I revived minutes later, I was in a lot of pain. There was no elevator, so Dennis and Pastor Chen carried me down four flights of stairs. They carefully put me into a taxi and rushed me to the hospital emergency room. After the doctor examined me, he informed us that I was pregnant with an ectopic pregnancy and one of my fallopian tubes had burst. Consequently, they rushed me immediately into surgery. I lost the baby and the fallopian tube, but they saved my life.

Then a second miracle occurred. Many women who lose a fallopian tube find it very difficult afterwards to become pregnant. But not long after my recovery from surgery, I became pregnant again. In 1973, our daughter, Sharon, was born; and her brother, Michael, followed in 1976. Sharon and her husband, Samuel, who is Chinese, are now the senior pastors of the church that Dennis planted in 1969. Ethnically, both our children are Caucasian, but in every other way they are Chinese. Both were born in Hong Kong and have lived there all their lives. They grew up speaking Chinese, and only as young adults, studied English. Even today, their Chinese is better than their English.

Dennis had been born for China. He had come to Hong Kong to invest his life, and not only his life, but the lives of his family as well. Indeed, our children have received a wonderful heritage, and it is reassuring to know that his legacy will live on.

CHAPTER TWELVE
GROWTH AND OPPOSITION

After Kathy and I married and she joined me in the work in Hong Kong, we saw steady, if not always rapid, growth in our church. Every week, it seemed we were seeing people saved, filled with the Spirit, healed of disease, or delivered of addiction or some other besetting sin. God was clearly at work in our midst, changing lives in the manner that only He can.

In 1975, God opened another door that considerably expanded our ministry outreach to the city of Hong Kong and brought even greater growth to our young and vibrant church. I was invited to become the chaplain of Hong Kong Christian College. The name of the school was somewhat misleading. First, even though it was called a "college," it was actually a school for primary, middle school, and high school-age students. Second, despite the word "Christian" in the school's name, there was very little about the school that was Christian. Except for the school principal and one teacher named Ralph Bullock, a missionary with the Apostolic Faith Church who had come to Hong Kong in 1933 with a vision to teach the Chinese people, none of the faculty or staff were Christians; and the only Christians among the student body were a few who happened to come from a Christian family background.

Hong Kong Christian College was founded by a wealthy Chinese

Christian businessman—a Mr. Ling. He was not a pastor and had no affiliation with any particular church, but he had a heart to preach the Gospel. Among other business interests, Mister Ling also owned the International Hotel in Hong Kong, which, although gone today, was a major and prosperous enterprise in those days.

Every student attended Bible class and was required to also attend assembly once a week. Because of the size of the student body and the fact that they were divided by grade level, a total of eight assemblies were held weekly. One day in 1975, a local pastor arranged for me to speak at one of the assemblies. I had been in Hong Kong only a few years, yet many people seemed to be impressed with the fluency of my Cantonese, especially Mr. Ling. After the assembly, he came to me and asked if I would be willing to serve as the school's chaplain. This meant, primarily, that I would be responsible for eight weekly assemblies, in addition to counseling with students, faculty, or staff as the need arose. I immediately recognized the opportunity that God was giving me to expand my influence and reach more people with the Gospel, so I said yes.

The assembly was the first school activity each morning, and was held in a huge hall that could seat probably up to one thousand people. It usually lasted an hour, sometimes a little longer, and I was given permission to hold the meetings in any way I deemed appropriate. We would start by singing the school song, and then I would lead everyone in singing some hymns. After the singing, I would read the Bible and preach. It was just like having church every day of the week.

At the time I became chaplain, our church was enjoying the fruits of our labors in a part of Hong Kong that had a reputation for being a very difficult area. Yet because the Lord was directing our steps, the church grew; and in those early years, we saw a wonderful harvest. We regularly went door-to-door and passed out tracts to everyone we could. We witnessed for Christ whenever we had the opportunity, and continuously made ourselves a visible presence in the community.

Becoming chaplain of Hong Kong Christian College introduced me to a new area of work where I had never specifically planned to go—student ministry. Because of my involvement in the chaplaincy at the school from 1975 to 1981, our church then started and continued a student fellowship. Eventually, so many came that it led to the physical relocation of our church. We decided to rent a building on Mody Road in the Tsim Sha Tsui District and move the church there, because the school was located in that District and because most of the students also lived there.

It was quite a step of faith. The church had been prospering in its present location, but I felt a strong leading of the Lord to relocate to Kowloon. However, the building we rented, like most of the commercial rental property in Hong Kong, had not been designed with a church in mind. The space had many pillars and was divided into numerous small rooms. Most landlords of such properties were amenable to the idea of knocking out pillars that were not critical for structural integrity and tearing down interior walls that were not load-bearing walls in order to create a larger interior space. Usually, the main condition to this arrangement was to restore the space to its original condition when vacating the property, or paying the landlord so that he or she could restore it. When we rented our building in Kowloon, we removed all the interior walls so we could have the largest possible space for worship.

In that location, our church grew from several dozen to several hundred people, most of them students, and often their families as well. Students were coming to the church at every meeting and getting saved. It was a time of great harvest of young souls, who were the future of Hong Kong…and China.

Another advantage of being the chaplain of Hong Kong Christian College was the freedom to do anything I felt God leading me to do. If the institution had been an affiliated school, such as a Baptist school or an Assembly of God school, I would have been somewhat bound by the traditions and expectations of those groups. But because the school was unaffiliated with any specific denomination, I had complete freedom. I was the only preacher, and I could invite other speakers as I saw fit. I could pray for the sick or teach on the Holy Spirit or lead revival songs and get the people clapping. For six years, I ministered, week after week to 3,000 people. Those students heard the Gospel and then shared it at home with their families. Because I was so strategically placed, I and our church had a tremendous impact, especially in that part of the city. Only the Lord could have opened such a unique door.

At one point, a man named Paul Sarchet-Waller joined our church. Paul was from England and had originally come with the hope of accomplishing mission work through one of the Pentecostal churches in the city. Somehow, he had met a missionary in Jamaica who recommended and worked through this particular church. When Paul arrived in Hong Kong, however, he discovered that the Pentecostal church did not actually want to have anything to do with "Pentecostal." Even though it called itself Pentecostal, the church was not truly open to the work of the Holy Spirit. In addition, the pastor was not really interested in Paul being there, and gave him no opportunities to preach.

So Paul eventually accepted a job teaching English at the Diocesan Boys College, a highly acclaimed school in Hong Kong, which was affiliated with the Anglican Church in England. Subsequently, Paul's association with our church drew in some of his students from the Diocesan Boys College. The graduates of this school are virtually assured of securing top jobs in government or business. In addition, in those days, the general level of education, moral standards, and work habits were much higher everywhere in the world than they are today. Many schools today, particularly in America, sad to say, graduate people who cannot even read well enough to fill out a simple job application. But back in the 1970s—and still true today—the standards in Hong Kong were higher. People worked harder and there was much more competition. Anyone who did not earn good grades could not move upward to the next level.

Between Hong Kong Christian College and Diocesan Boys College, we attracted some top-notch students, who became the foundation of our church. Even today, the pastor of one of our branch churches is a former student of Diocesan Boys College, who was saved through our ministry and discipled in our church.

A number of other former students are involved with our ministry in one way or another, and there are even more who are ministering overseas. The Lord directed many successful people into our midst, those with prosperous careers and high incomes, who married similar people and raised families. In this way, the Lord blessed our church with tremendous growth and strength, both spiritually and financially.

As wonderful and exciting as it was to have our church grow and see lost people saved and filled with the Holy Spirit, that harvest did not come without a price. From the very beginning we labored in the face of opposition from many different quarters. Whenever God starts to work in a mighty way among a people group, you can be sure that the enemy will rise to the attack; and when he does, he is relentless. It is bad enough when opposition comes from the worldly arena, from people who are opposed to God and all that He stands for; it is even worse when opposition arises from fellow believers, from churches, from the very people you would expect and hope to support you.

That's how it was with us in the early days. We actually faced more opposition and resistance to our work from other churches in Hong Kong, especially other evangelical churches, than we did from unbelievers. At times, the opposition was so intense that we might well have become discouraged enough to give up and quit had the Lord not sustained us by His presence and by His miraculous workings in our midst. As I said before, when I first began my ministry in Hong Kong in 1969, there were very few Spirit-filled churches in the city. In most cases, even the churches that began with a Pentecostal background and tradition came to deny the active work of the Holy Spirit, and were Pentecostal in name only. So when I started Revival Christian Church, with its emphasis on not only the Gospel message of salvation through faith in Christ, but also on the baptism, gifts, and work of the Holy Spirit, many other churches in Hong Kong were quick to condemn us as a cult.

For example, there was a Christian Missionary Alliance Church in Hong Kong that owned a bookstore right across the street from Hong Kong Christian College. Out of all the thousands of books in stock at that store, the one they chose to display prominently in the front window was a book entitled True and False Tongues. Many students undoubtedly noticed that book as they walked by that store every day on their way to school, and probably more than a few bought it. So there I was, as the school chaplain preaching Jesus and teaching on the baptism of the Holy Spirit and speaking in tongues, while across the street was a Christian bookstore advertising a book that attacked everything I was teaching with regard to the Holy Spirit. Sometimes it was tough, but we stood strong and refused to back down under the opposition. On another occasion, one of the female members of our church became a student at the Assembly of God Bible College, and reported to me that the college was teaching its students that our church was a cult.

What hurt most was when the opposition hit especially close to home. Our son, Michael, was attending the United Christian College in Hong Kong when the principal decided to speak to the entire student body one day. Knowing that Michael (who was in the audience) was my son, he proceeded to denounce me and our church. At that time, our church was located on Prince Edward Road, very close to the school. The principal said, "There is a church nearby that is called Revival Christian Church. The pastor is Dennis Balcombe. This church is a cult; none of you should ever go there."

Can you imagine how our son felt to hear his father, his church, his family, and by extension, himself, denounced so publicly, especially in front of friends and classmates? People in our church often came up and asked me, "Why are they saying these things about us? Why are they calling us a cult, and saying that we teach heresy?"

My only answer…"I don't really know. We are simply teaching what the Bible says."

One pastor actually tried to stop people from coming to our meetings, and he also insisted that our church was a cult and that we were preaching and teaching heresy, simply because I spoke in tongues. When I heard about it, I decided to try to meet with him in the hope of fostering Christian brotherhood and understanding. After all, Jesus said we should dialogue with our adversaries and try to make peace with them.

So I went to meet with this man, and one of the first things he said to me was, "I want to test your spirit," referring to First John 4:1 (NIV), which says: "Dear friends, do not believe every spirit, but test the spirits to see whether they are from God, because many false prophets have gone out into the world." He then asked me, "Do you confess that Jesus Christ, the Son of God, has come in the flesh?"

"Yes, I do," I responded.

He appeared quite frustrated over my answer. Apparently, he had expected me to manifest a demon, or to deny that Jesus was fully human as well as fully divine. In the Scripture that he was referencing, the Apostle John writes about a Gnostic sect who had arisen in his day as false prophets. This sect taught that the physical, material world was evil, and therefore, the Son of God could not truly have taken on physical flesh, but only appeared to be human.

I still don't quite understand why this man chose to test me in this way, and with this Scripture. I assume he wanted me to declare that Jesus was not the Son of God or that He had not come in the flesh. But nonetheless, no matter what a person actually believes, anyone can confess that Jesus came in the flesh. That doesn't prove anyone's true spirit. Even the antichrist can say that Jesus came in the flesh. In any case, that is how he decided to question me, and consequently, he became extremely upset when I affirmed Jesus the same way he did. Frankly, he was so set in his mind that I was preaching heresy, that he decided not to believe me. He concluded, "You are just saying that with your mouth; you don't really believe it in your spirit."

"Brother," I said, "do you have any gifts of the Spirit? Do you have the word of knowledge? How could you possibly know what is in my spirit? And besides, you are misusing this Scripture. If you want to know my spirit, look at the fruit. People are getting saved in our church every week. When I began as chaplain of Hong Kong Christian College, almost none of the students were Christians. Since then, we have seen hundreds of students get saved and baptized. They are now Christians. Even if they do not go to your church, they are still going to Heaven. And whether they speak in tongues or not, they are still going to Heaven."

I did not stop there. I told him that he was actually doing more harm than good. Traditionally, the Chinese people have a great fear of evil spirits. They believe that when you die you become a ghost. If you die violently, you become a violent ghost. They conduct many different religious ceremonies with the purpose of trying to appease these spirits. In traditional Chinese culture, almost everyone believes in the supernatural. This pastor stated publicly and often that there were some tongues that truly were of God, but that most tongues were false, and of the devil. He went so far as to say, "If you go to Pastor Balcombe's church and receive the Holy Spirit, you may actually end up receiving another spirit altogether." Because so many people were afraid of evil spirits, quite a few who had been attending our church stopped coming because of what this pastor said.

If it had just been a matter of some people leaving our church and going somewhere else, it would not have been so bad. But as I said to that pastor, "Don't think that if people stop going to my church over this that they will start going to your church, or somewhere else. They won't. They will never touch Christianity again. They will never believe in Jesus again. They are afraid. You have scared them off. In the end, they will go nowhere."

He and I had quite a long discussion, but to no avail. I did not get very far with him, and he certainly did not persuade me.

This pastor is still preaching, he is well-known, and he still remains opposed to the teaching of the baptism of the Holy Spirit and speaking in tongues, although he is not as forceful as he once was. I believe he has realized he cannot deny the simple fact that today, most of the churches in Hong Kong are very open to the Holy Spirit, and the vast majority do speak in tongues.

However, that change did not occur overnight. It developed slowly and gradually through the 1980s and early 1990s, but significantly advanced, ironically, after the 1997 transfer of Hong Kong's sovereignty back to the jurisdiction of mainland China. Before the arrival of that landmark date, many evangelical pastors, church leaders, and missionaries in Hong Kong, especially those who were not

Spirit-filled, left, because they had no faith that Hong Kong would be safe after China took over. The general assumption in the Western church was that the communists would come into Hong Kong and close the churches, arrest the pastors, and persecute the Chinese believers. Very few expected the concept of "one country, two systems" to survive. We, however, were confident that it would. We continued to believe God's promise that China was going to open up and that Hong Kong would influence and change China…not the other way around. Furthermore, Great Britain had given Hong Kong sovereignty, which meant that they could choose to do whatever they wanted. And that is exactly what happened. In the years since the transfer in 1997, we have gained even more freedom to preach the Gospel and teach about the Holy Spirit than we had before. In every other way, our freedom in Hong Kong today is no different than it was before the transfer.

The departure of the non-Pentecostal evangelicals before the transfer left the field wide open for Pentecostal preaching and teaching, because Pentecostals were just about the only ones who remained. Once the older pastors and leaders left, all who remained were young people, who were not concerned with what had happened in China in 1949 when the communists took over. Those young believers were interested in only one outcome—they wanted to be successful in the ministry, and they wanted to minister to their own people. As a result, today most of the churches in Hong Kong are Spirit-filled.

But in those early years, we faced much opposition. Yet our church continued to grow. As time went on and we continued to see students saved, we eventually outgrew our building on Mody Road. So it was time to move again. We found another rental property on Nathan Road, shaped like an L, which was 5,000 square feet—about the size we needed, but with an unusual history. Although it had been vacant for a couple of years, it had been previously used as a brothel, divided into a series of small rooms, where people had provided various sexual services. At some point, the building had also served as a nightclub. Someone who was involved in the mafia or the Chinese Triad had even been killed there. Consequently, the building had been vacant for several years because the Chinese people are very superstitious. When we rented the property for a greatly reduced rate, there were still bullet holes in the walls. It was a picturesque place with a sad and sordid history, but now we had claimed it for Jesus.

The first task we faced was to knock out the walls of 30 small rooms to create one large space. Then we needed to add air conditioning and proper ventilation. Because we could not afford to hire a company to perform these renovations, we did the work ourselves. Interestingly, in the course of remodeling, we found a locked safe that had been left behind. Naturally, we wondered what was inside, and we dreamed, half jokingly, that the safe contained a million dollars. After drilling and hammering, we were able to break it open. Alas...we found...no money. Just some pictures of prostitutes...and we prayed for them.

As the renovations progressed, we accumulated a substantial amount of waste materials, and to get rid of this waste, we used an old English truck that was in very poor condition, with very unreliable brakes. Driving the truck fell to me, because in those days most of the people in our church did not have a driver's license.

One night, several of us took the truck to the dump, and while there, a heavy rain from a typhoon came pouring down. Instantly, the ground was soaked and became very muddy, and somehow an iron bar became entangled with one of the axles of the truck. For a long time, no matter how hard we tried, we could not get it out. At one point, we even crawled under the truck to work, with all the rotting garbage, dead animals, and who knows what else lying around.

Finally, we got the truck free and drove to the gate to exit, only to discover that it was locked. We asked the people in charge to let us out, but they would not do so. They claimed that the sign clearly stated that the dump closed at 10:00 p.m. Of course, it was much later than that. I tried to reason with them that the purpose of a lock is to keep people out, not to keep people in, but they would not budge. We could have walked and left the truck behind...and that is exactly what I told those who were with me to do. I decided to stay behind, because I knew that if I left, someone would take the truck...I stayed at the dump all night.

That was the way it was—we did whatever we had to do. We were Christians; we were serving the Lord. No service was too great—or too menial. And the people appreciated it. And at all times, we emphasized preaching the Gospel.

Because Nathan Road was a main street, our new location there gave us excellent visibility. We got into the habit of having a communal meal together every Sunday afternoon after the service, which was extremely popular with students, because most of them had very little money. We did not have much money either, and it was not cheap to serve a meal for that many people, but we did it anyway, trusting that the Lord would provide and that people would pitch in as they were able.

In addition, very early on, even while we were still at our first location, we started Shiloh Bible College. Although it was a local church Bible school rather than an accredited institution of higher learning, many students came. In fact, it was not unusual to have classes with 60, 70, or even 80 people. These were people who had never attended a formal Bible college, and in most cases could not afford to go. Shiloh Bible College continues even today, although it is not full time.

Some of my most cherished memories are of those times when Kathy and I stood on a mountain in the northern part of Hong Kong at the border that overlooked China and prayed for that country. China was my vision and focus, and it became Kathy's vision and focus as well. I continued to affirm, "One day, China will open. When it does, we will go in. And our church will go in." My vision was to have the whole church involved in China. Revival Christian Church might be physically located in Hong Kong, but our mission is China. Our church has always been a mission-minded church, just as I have always been a mission-minded pastor.

From the time I brought Kathy to Hong Kong in 1971 until 1978, she and I went regularly to that mountain. Many people thought we were crazy. "China is never going to open up," they insisted. They thought we were out of our minds even to suggest such an idea. Even many former missionaries to China, who had been kicked out by the communists, were saying that it was the endtimes and that China had had her day. Now the door was closed and Jesus was coming again. They assumed that China was doomed—it was a very sad outlook. But Kathy and I knew that China would open up. Indeed, Pastor David Schoch, a well-known prophet at that time, and others had prophesied over me to that effect. More importantly, however, is that God Himself had spoken to me and said, "China will open up, and you will go in."

China opened up to the outside world in 1978. And we went in.

CHAPTER THIRTEEN
FIELDS WHITE UNTO HARVEST

The opening of China in 1978 ushered in a whole new dimension of our work and ministry. Everything we did in Hong Kong those first ten years, everything we experienced, everything we accomplished—the labor, the hardships, the joy, the sorrow—all of it was God's way of preparing us for even greater ministry in China.

In those early years, all we had was the promise from God that China would open up one day, but we had no idea when it would occur. God kept His own counsel concerning the date. Our job was to be faithful to the task God had given us—to preach the Gospel of Jesus Christ to the lost, plant and grow a church, and teach on the baptism of the Holy Spirit. We did not know when we would go into China, but we knew that our ministry in Hong Kong and the church we started there would in time become the base of operations for future ministry into China.

Now it was happening. The Gang of Four was gone; a new, more open regime was in power; and the door was opening. As we stood on that mountainside, we raised our hands over that great land that lay before us and prayed for the Chinese people and for the work that we would soon undertake there. God had already prepared the way. Our church was growing and thriving, and our people were ready to go in, ready to fulfill all that God had promised and all that He had brought us this far to do. China was our destiny, and we were going in!

When the communists under Mao Zedong defeated the nationalists under Chiang Kai-shek in 1948, the nationalists retreated to Taiwan, where they set up a "government in exile." Mainland China came under communist control, all Westerners had to leave, the "Bamboo Curtain" fell, and the West lost contact.

Then, during the decade of 1967 to 1976, China came under the control of radicals, sometimes referred to as the "Gang of Four," who initiated a reign of terror under the benign title, "Cultural Revolution." After the death of Chairman Mao on September 9, 1976, a power struggle ensued between the Gang of Four (which included Chairman Mao's widow) and more reform-minded communists led by Deng Xiaoping. It took over a year for Deng to gain enough power to begin his "open door policy." Eventually, the Gang of Four were brought down and arrested. Once Deng consolidated his control, China opened to tourism, businessmen, and foreign investment. Economic policy began to shift from a centrally-controlled economy to a market-based economy. This shift has continued until today China boasts one of the largest, strongest, and most robust economies in the world.

Our first clue in Hong Kong that a change was coming appeared during the first week of January 1978, when we read in the local newspaper that the state-controlled "China Travel Service" was now arranging tours in which "foreign guests" (Westerners) could participate. I was one of the first to join such a tour, and entered China for the first time around the second week of January 1978.

It was an unforgettable experience. We took the train from the central train station in Hong Kong and went to the border. After crossing the border from Hong Kong into China, we took the Chinese train from Shenzhen, the border city, to Guangzhou, the next big city up the line. As a result of the Cultural Revolution and the policies of the communists, China was then an extremely poor and backward nation. The people dressed mostly in the blue or gray workers' clothes of that period. Like the men, the women dressed in pants, and most had short hair and wore no makeup. Few people wore wristwatches, and other types of jewelry were very scarce. Food and clothes continued to be rationed; restaurants were hard to find, and the few that were in operation were open only certain hours for breakfast, lunch, and dinner. Most people shopped at large government department stores, as private shops and businesses were still quite rare.

I was, of course, part of an official tour, in which a Chinese travel agency took us to visit communes, hospitals, schools, and factories, where communist leaders lectured about the initial great achievements of the Communist Party in bringing China out of the poverty that had been widespread under the leadership of the former Nationalist Party government. They then denounced the subsequent disastrous polices of the Gang of Four and the brutal repression under the Cultural Revolution, and they also were quick to emphasize that China now had an open-door policy.

As a group we walked on the streets, went to the local parks, and visited department stores. My group included about 20 Westerners dressed in colorful clothes, sporting various modern hair styles, and carrying cameras around their necks. Wherever we went, huge crowds gathered around and simply stared at us. They had seen nothing like us in 30 years.

Because I spoke fluent Cantonese, the language of Guangzhou (the first city we went to), I began a conversation with some in the crowd. Behind me was a huge poster displaying, "Down with the American imperialists," so I asked them what they thought about Americans. Someone in the crowd shouted out, "Actually, that is only government propaganda. We never believe what the government says, and we don't believe that. We know the Americans sacrificed their lives to free us from Japanese occupation. Actually we love all Westerners, especially the Americans." This response shocked me; it was totally unexpected. And it was then that I began to realize that although China as a nation had been closed politically for 30 years, the hearts of the people were still quite open.

Now that I was in China after so many years of waiting, I took every possible opportunity to share my faith. Many of the Chinese people I spoke to told me that they knew of Christians somewhere or the location of a Christian church that had been opened at one time. (But it would not be until 1979 that the Religious Affairs Bureau would begin to reopen the Three-Self Patriotic Churches or Association.) I had no idea how to contact Chinese Christians or even where I might find them.

Throughout 1978 I took several short trips into the country, and all the time I was asking the Lord what type of ministry I should become involved with there, not knowing where to begin. Finally, I consulted a brother in our church, Simon Lam, who had escaped from China by swimming to Hong Kong, and who is now a pastor of a branch Chinese church in Castro Valley, California. I asked Simon if he knew of any churches in China.

Simon, at the time of his escape, had never attended church meetings, although his parents were Christian. And even at the time I talked to him, his father was living in Guangzhou, but still did not dare go to Christian meetings. After a few additional inquiries, I discovered that there were many Christians in China, but they desperately needed Bibles. Specifically, I was told about a certain area in Guangxi Province (next to Guangdong Province) where 40,000 Christians met regularly in many home churches, but had only one full Bible among them.

I then knew what I would do. I immediately started to notify churches in the States and around the world with this message: "China is now open. We don't know when it might close again. The Christians there desperately need Bibles. Please come to Hong Kong and support us in delivering Bibles to China."

In those days, there were virtually no custom checks in place for foreigners going into China; and within months, hundreds of Western believers arrived every month to take Bibles into the nation. From that point until the end of 1981, when customs checks for Western tourists were finally instituted, thousands of Bibles were delivered into Guangzhou. News spread quickly all over China through the vast house church network system. Subsequently, leaders came to Guangzhou on a daily basis to pick up these Bibles and then ship them to their own house churches all across the country.

As early as 1979, I was able to meet with many key leaders of the main house church movements all over China. They, in turn, wanted me to visit them in their rural churches…but this was far too dangerous for them and actually impossible for me to do. In those early days, Western entry into China was gained by way of either signing up for an organized tour, or applying for a business visa. In addition, only a few major cities were open, and we were required to obtain a separate visa for each one of those cities. We also were required to stay and register in state-approved hotels. That meant that whenever we left the country, they would have easily been able to check where we stayed each night, because the information had been documented.

So, because of these restrictions, for many years we met with house church leaders only in hotel rooms or restaurants of the major cities we were allowed to visit, including Beijing, Shanghai, Kunming, and Xian. In addition, I invited key Western pastors and church leaders from around the world to participate in these tours, and we all were thrilled and challenged to hear the testimonies of these men and women of faith.

The question the Chinese people asked me most often was, "How is it that you are not the head of a large church organization, or a wealthy and influential Western church? Why are you the pastor of an ordinary local church in Hong Kong? And why do you deliver tens of thousands of Bibles to us each month? What is the reason?"

I told them, "Yes, I am just an ordinary person and we have an ordinary church. Yet we are filled with the Holy Spirit, have great faith, pray and fast, and know many Spirit-filled churches all over the world. When I told them about your need, they all responded by sending couriers and financial support so we could purchase these Bibles."

"We have heard about the baptism of the Holy Spirit," they responded, "and know a few who have had this experience. But we do not know much about this teaching." Their religious background had been gained mostly through an evangelical mission started by Hudson Taylor—the China Inland Mission. So, we prayed for many leaders in hotel rooms and restaurants, and they were baptized in the Spirit. They then took this anointing back to their churches in Henan,

Anhui, Shandong, Zhejiang, and many other provinces. Eventually, we were able to travel to other cities without restrictions, although it always remained dangerous for a Christian missionary to go to a rural area.

In spite of the risks, however, the Christians in Henan invited me to their workers' training meetings in the mid-1980s. So, I took the train from Guangzhou to Zhengzhou (the capital of Henan), arriving late in the evening. From there we rented a vehicle to southern Henan, where we arrived about 3:00 a.m. At that time there was no electric power in these rural areas, so we walked for another hour through many dark villages to the meeting place. As we approached each village, visible only by lantern light, I was amazed to hear the sounds, not of farm animals, but of people praying with great intensity.

Entering the gate in the large courtyard, I saw hundreds of preachers, all of whom looked like local farmers, on their knees crying out to God in fervent prayer and intercession, tears flowing down their faces. They immediately took me into a building, which was nothing more than a small home that had been converted to a meeting place. Inside, there were at least 200 people, crowded into one small room, filling it from wall to wall. Many others remained outside.

"How many people are at this meeting?" I asked. I was shocked at the answer. Altogether there were about 800 preachers, representing 400 churches. Each church had been allowed to send only two preachers to the meeting. And because most churches had an attendance of several hundred believers, this group represented over 100,000 Christians. A large percentage of the congregation could not even crowd into the room, but stood outside close to the open doors and windows, listening as I spoke.

At 6:30 a.m., after two hours of intense prayer, they asked me to speak.

"How long?" I asked, expecting to give a greeting or share a testimony for a few minutes.

"Oh no, not for a few minutes," they corrected me. "It is now 6:30 a.m. We will have a breakfast break at 8:00 a.m., a lunch break at 12:00 noon, and a dinner break at 6:00 p.m. The meeting will end somewhere around 9:30 or 10:00 p.m. None of the meal breaks will be longer than 30 to 45 minutes. The rest of the time we want you to minister to us. We will be here for three whole days, and then go to another district for another three days. We have arranged the next two weeks for you."

I had not come prepared for that kind of ministry. I had no notes, no camera, no books—nothing but the Bible. But as I got up to speak, the Holy Spirit anointing came, the Bible came alive, and I had no problem preaching to 800 people for ten hours a day. Every two to three hours I would take a break, we would sing a song, and I would pray for the leaders to be filled with the Holy Spirit.

There were reservations on the part of some leaders regarding both my doctrine about the Holy Spirit and what actually happened when God moved. They had been taught by the missionaries that these gifts of the Spirit had ceased with the deaths of the apostles in the first century. On the other hand, they had also seen many miracles already in their ministry, so it was not that hard to accept that tongues might also be something God was giving people today. Some leaders became frightened when hundreds started speaking in tongues, dancing, crying, shouting, or falling. At times, they would attempt to stop what was happening by singing a song…but without success. We all know that once God begins to move in a meeting, nobody can stop Him!

Within months there was not only no more opposition, but these Henan preachers were arranging for me to travel all over China to preach this same message. Why? After they received the baptism in the Holy Spirit, great boldness came upon them, and miracles began to follow their preaching. Each group who opened to this message saw tremendous revival, and their numbers multiplied everywhere.

I persevered in this ministry until May 1995, at which time the Chinese government revoked my visa for seven years. So, for seven years, I could not enter China. Nevertheless, ministry there forged ahead as others went in, including people from our own church in Hong Kong as well as visitors from outside. Deliveries of thousands of Bibles also continued. Then, in January 2003, my visa was renewed, and I have carried on the same ministry to this day. The most significant difference now is in addition to house churches, I am ministering a significant amount of time in the official Three-Self Patriotic Churches or Association. These people also want revival and the Holy Spirit.

For the last 42 years in Hong Kong and the last 33 in China, I have counted it a blessed privilege to be able to serve the Lord in this great nation, and among the gracious, wonderful Chinese people.

Do you not say, "There are still four months and then comes the harvest"? Behold, I say to you, lift up your eyes and look at the fields, for they are already white for harvest! (John 4:35 NKJV)

Then He said to His disciples, "The harvest truly is plentiful, but the laborers are few. Therefore pray the Lord of the harvest to send out laborers into His harvest" (Matthew 9:37-38 NKJV).

CHAPTER FOURTEEN
WHY CHINA

By this point, it should be clear that I have a passion for China, and Kathy shares that passion as well. We love the Chinese people. We think in Chinese. We speak Chinese...more than we speak English. We have immersed ourselves in the Chinese culture and society for the last 40 years. In virtually every way except our physical, ethnic characteristics, we are Chinese.

Why have we done this? Why would two young Americans essentially turn their backs on their own culture and society to embrace those of the Chinese people? Why invest our lives among a people, who, although wonderful and beautiful in their own right, are so different from ourselves in so many ways?

The simplest answer, and the most significant, is that God has called us to this life and work. We are blessed to be among that great company throughout history whom God has set apart to carry the Good News of salvation in Jesus Christ into the farthest corners of the world. There is nothing extraordinary about either Kathy or me. We are ordinary people who have been rescued from sin and death by Jesus and now are sold out to Him. We are ordinary people in the service of an extraordinary God.

God has always had a heart for the nations. Thousands of years ago, He called Abraham to Himself and promised to make of him a great nation, the nation of Israel, through whom would come One who would bless the nations of the earth. That One is Jesus Christ, the Son of God, born of a virgin, sacrificed on a cross to bear in His own body the judgment of God for our sins, buried and raised again to life in victory over sin and death.

Jesus Himself said, "For God so loved the world that He gave His only begotten Son, that whoever believes in Him should not perish but have everlasting life" (John 3:16 NKJV). Before He went to the cross, Jesus commissioned His own followers to take up their own part in God's eternal plan for the nations: "Go into all the world and preach the gospel to every creature" (Mark 16:15b NKJV). Matthew's version of this Great Commission is more familiar to most Christians: "Go therefore and make disciples of all the nations, baptizing them in the name of the Father and of the Son and of the Holy Spirit, teaching them to observe all things that I have commanded you; and lo, I am with you always, even to the end of the age" (Matt. 28:19-20 NKJV).

In the original Greek of the New Testament, the word "Go" in Matthew 28:19 is continuing action; it literally means, "as you go." This means that we are to make disciples "as we go" through the affairs of daily life. Making disciples is the calling of every Christian, whether it means going halfway around the world, or just across the street.

Before He ascended into Heaven, Jesus gave to His disciples one final promise, and it too relates to God's plan for the nations: "You shall receive power when the Holy Spirit has come upon you; and you shall be witnesses to Me in Jerusalem, and in all Judea and Samaria, and to the end of the earth" (Acts 1:8 NKJV).

This verse is an apt description of our ministry. For 40 years, Kathy and I have been witnesses to Jesus Christ, in the power of the Holy Spirit, to the end of the earth. Our particular "end of the earth" has been Hong Kong, and since 1978, China. From the beginning, Hong Kong has been a strategic location in God's plan to reach the whole of China with the Gospel. Even the earliest pastors and missionaries who traveled to Hong Kong in the mid-1800s claimed that the city would be a base from which to evangelize China until Jesus returns. They were absolutely right. For over 150 years, Hong Kong has been somewhat of a headquarters and a launching point for Gospel mission work in the interior of China, as well as in the coastal cities. And despite all the so-called prophets who predicted doom and destruction for Hong Kong and its churches after the 1997 handover to Chinese sovereignty, Hong Kong's status as a missionary base remains the same.

In fact, Hong Kong today is freer than it was even under British rule. Actually, Hong Kong is freer than any other place on earth. This is a miracle that most people in the West do not understand. People in Hong Kong have more control over their own personal and business finances than those who live in most other countries. Certainly, there are financial laws and regulations; however, it is easier to start a business in Hong Kong than anywhere else in the world. Anyone with 20 to 50 U.S. dollars can start a business in Hong Kong and be up and running in a couple of days.

Strong regulations, coupled with almost zero illegal activity, make Hong Kong a choice environment for success and prosperity. Generally speaking, business operations run very efficiently here. This achievement began in the late 1970s, when an independent commission against corruption was established in Hong Kong. As a result, there is now less financial crime in Hong Kong than there is in America. When I first came to Hong Kong, it was overrun with fraudulent commercial and economic activities; consequently, this commission was established to deal with dishonest and crooked schemes. It is almost like a second government in its own right; it operates as an independent entity and answers neither to the police nor to the general Hong Kong government. Anyone who suspects an individual or a business of committing a financial crime can make an anonymous report to the commission. Subsequently, the commission will investigate.

If the commission finds that the person or business being investigated possesses assets that exceed what their income should allow, the commission will lay down a charge of financial misconduct. Let's say that you earned $100,000 a year and also owned a 10 million-dollar mansion. The commission would contact you and ask you to explain how you could afford such a property on your reported income. If you cannot justify or prove the honest acquisition of your possessions, they can declare that you acquired your assets through deceptive methods, and you would go to jail. Because of the existence of this commission, corruption in Hong Kong has been eliminated by about 99 percent.

In addition, Hong Kong also enjoys complete freedom of religion. Christians can go freely into public schools, and even preach if the principal allows it. We can pray. We can pass out Bibles. We can stand on the street corner and share the Gospel without having to register or acquire a permit. We can go into prisons and hospitals. We can preach on television and radio. We can start churches without having to register—although registering is beneficial because it provides tax exempt status.

Income taxes are very low in Hong Kong; the highest tax rate is 15 percent. Furthermore, there is virtually no limit to the amount of charitable contributions that can be deducted from your taxes. Everyone in Hong Kong does pay an indirect income tax, because the land is auctioned out. Land is very expensive in Hong Kong, because there is so little of it. By paying rent, everyone in Hong Kong pays into this indirect tax.

Even now, Hong Kong is a tremendous base to reach the people in China. Thousands of Chinese from the mainland visit Hong Kong every year, and many of those who come are from underground house churches. Although they cannot be granted a passport to leave China, they can travel to Hong Kong without a passport or even a visa. The only documentation they need is a photo ID card that everyone in China carries by law. By presenting this ID card to the local police station, each person can obtain a permit to visit Hong Kong for seven days.

Our church and others in Hong Kong capitalize on this opportunity by holding many meetings across a given seven-day period, so that these house-church Christians can receive teaching and ministry in a free and open setting before returning to their homes in the cities or rural districts of China.

Many Christians had assumed that the handover of Hong Kong to Chinese jurisdiction in 1997 would mean a closed door to the Gospel. Yet the exact opposite has been true; we are freer today in Hong Kong than we were prior to 1997. Only God could have orchestrated something like that. China is an open door, and Hong Kong is the gateway.

Someone might still ask, "Why China? After all, Dennis, there are many other nations of the world that are important, whose people still need to hear the Gospel. What is so significant about China?"

First, China is home to one fifth of the world's population. At 1.3 billion people, China is the most populous nation in the world. Only India, with a population of approximately 1.1 billion, comes anywhere close to rivaling China. As these figures show, the human population is exploding in Asia, and that alone is enough to make China (as well as India) strategic in any plans for world evangelization.

Second, China is important because it has one of the largest, strongest, and fastest-growing economies in the world. Although China is a communist nation, it operates a modified but highly independent free-market economy that has taken the world by storm over the last 20 to 30 years. Today, China is the world's largest manufacturer and exporter of goods of all kinds, from toys to clothing to electronics and computer software. Because of its robust economy and heavy investments in international markets, China has become a primary lender to many nations, including the United States. World economic power is shifting from the West to the East, and many analysts predict that within a generation or so, China will be the world's dominant economy.

China is also important because of the spiritual character of its people. Despite the officially atheistic position of the current communist Chinese government, the Chinese have always been a deeply spiritual race. Its culture is one of the oldest in the world, dating back to ancient times. In fact, Chinese civilization is the only ancient civilization that has managed to survive continuously and unbroken into the present day. Chinese culture was well developed as early as 1,500 years before Christ; and by that date, the written Chinese language already included as many as 2,500 different and distinct characters.

The Shang dynasty, the earliest known of China's major dynasties, flourished in the Yellow River valley from approximately 1700-1100 BC, the same time period during which other great Middle Eastern civilizations were arising and thriving along the Nile, Tigris, and Euphrates rivers. Writing and wheeled chariots both were also in use during this time.

However, as powerful as it was, the Shang dynasty eventually faded, to be replaced by the Zhou dynasty, which reigned even longer, from approximately 1100-256 BC. The declining years of this great dynasty produced China's three greatest and revered philosophers: Confucius, Mencius, and Lao Tzu. Their philosophies grew out of the disorder and despair of the times in which they lived. And so thoroughly infused are their ideas into the culture of China today, that virtually every Chinese person is a reflection of the teachings of these three men.

Confucius is attributed with a concept called the "mandate of heaven," which is the principle that has been invoked as the reason behind every change of government in China since the days of the Zhou dynasty. The "mandate of heaven" states that any ruler who does not serve the people will be replaced by divine authorization. This is an amazing concept—that a ruler exists for the people, rather than the other way around. Many centuries would pass before the West would institute a similar idea, and would eliminate the "divine right of kings" in favor of the concept of a government that actually served the people. But that very principle was an established part of Chinese culture even before the birth of Christ.

While Confucius never spoke of belief in a personal God as we know, he did conceive of a moral force in the universe that he called "heaven" or "god." The term he used for this mysterious moral force, shen, is the same word used in the Chinese Bible. Perhaps his greatest contribution was what he called "intellectual democracy," the belief that all people should be permitted to think for themselves. It is impossible to overemphasize the influence of Confucius on Chinese culture and thought.

Mencius, although a disciple of Confucius, differed from his mentor in that he believed and taught that human nature is essentially good. This belief placed him in conflict with both Confucius and the Bible. He taught that man was self-sufficient, and he espoused an economic system similar to today's communism. It should be no surprise, then, that Chinese communists have adopted much of Mencius' philosophy, particularly the idea that because man is essentially good, there is no need for God.

Lao Tzu is credited with being the father of Taoism. However, there is no clear evidence that such a man ever lived. As a philosophy, Taoism is the opposite of communism, teaching that an absolute minimum of government is supreme, and that the goal is not an ideal society, but to live in harmony with nature. Because the way of the universe is inaction, non-action is preferable to action. In later times, Taoism degenerated into the worship of local gods, magic, and miracles, and even absorbed much from Indian Buddhism.

Because of the tremendous influence of these three philosophers, the Chinese people, in a sense, can be described as schizophrenic. Their dualistic nature is a combination of the restraints of Confucianism, and the free spirit of Taoism. They are welded to tradition, but are also able to flow with the currents of life and survive when others become extinct. In hard times, their Taoistic philosophy comes to the fore, and in times of prosperity, the Confucian ethic emerges. Confucianism has been the philosophy of the intellectual, while Taoism has been the philosophy of the uneducated peasant. Both philosophies then have flowed into each other, mingling to produce the Chinese person of today.

Many people in the West are familiar with this philosophical/spiritual aspect of the Chinese people. What most Westerners are unaware of, however (and most Chinese as well), is the very ancient tradition, predating Confucius, Mencius, Lao Tzu, and all the great Chinese dynasties, which says that the very earliest Chinese people were worshipers of the one true God.

Don Richardson, in his remarkable book, Eternity in Their Hearts, tells the story of the Lisu, a tribe of people occupying Yunnan Province of southwestern China, who have a very ancient tradition predicting the coming of a white-faced teacher who would restore to them a long-lost book of God in their own language. Richardson notes the remarkable fact that this tradition originated in a time when the Lisu did not even have an alphabet, much less a written language or any printed material! There were several tribes of people in neighboring sections of India and Burma, who had similar ancient traditions. Consequently, when white missionaries first contacted these people in the 19th century and preached the Gospel to them, the Lisu and other neighboring tribes turned to Christ by the thousands.

Even though the philosophies of Confucianism and Taoism, and religions such as Buddhism and, later, Islam have been expounded and practiced in China, the thread of that very ancient belief in the one true God has never really been lost, and has run as an undercurrent in the mind and spirit of the Chinese people for thousands of years. For this reason, when Chinese people hear the Gospel and place their faith in Jesus Christ, they are not just adopting a "foreign" religion; they are simply returning to their roots!

Unfortunately, the subjugation and exploitation of China by Western powers, primarily in the 19th and early 20th centuries, have caused deep resentment among the Chinese people, many of whom have associated Christianity with those who have exploited them, and thus have rejected it as a "Western" religion. Periodically, this resentment has boiled over into nationalist fervor and outright revolution, such as the Boxer rebellion, in which hundreds of Western missionaries and thousands of Chinese Christians were killed.

In spite of setbacks such as these, Christian missions in China flourished, until by the time of World War II, there was a strong and well-established Christian presence in China, although it was still a tiny minority compared to the total population of the country. After the war, the communists in China grew in power until, in 1949, under the leadership of Mao Zedong, they defeated the nationalist forces under Chiang Kai-shek and established a communist regime.

Chiang Kai-shek and other nationalists then fled to Taiwan and established a republican form of democracy there. Meanwhile, under the communists, Chinese churches were closed, Chinese Christians were persecuted, and Western missionaries were forced to leave. Those who did not were arrested, and some, such as Dr. Bill Wallace, a Baptist medical missionary, died in a Chinese prison. The so-called Bamboo Curtain fell, and China was closed to the West.

Under Chairman Mao, the Cultural Revolution instituted "reforms" to Chinese life and culture that were highly restrictive and oppressive to the Chinese people, particularly Christians. After Mao's death, the so-called Gang of Four, led by Mao's widow, continued his "reforms" with even more extreme repression until they were deposed in the mid-1970s. The new regime took a more open approach. Many of the oppressive and highly detrimental laws of the Cultural Revolution were discarded, and the Chinese government began to make overtures to the West for the first time in a generation. China began to open up.

During the 30 or so years of "silence" from China while Chairman Mao and his immediate successors ruled, one of the biggest questions in the minds of Western Christians was, "What of the church in China?" No one knew what had happened. Had the church in China thrived in spite of communist oppression, or had that oppression totally wiped out the Chinese church? Once Westerners were allowed into China again, the answer was soon revealed. Not only had the Chinese church survived during those years, but it had grown far beyond what anyone would have expected. But still, there were so many more Chinese to reach with the Gospel. And despite the phenomenal, even exponential, growth of the church in China in the years since, it is still true today.

Another question many Western Christians ask even today is, "Just how many Christians are there in China?" To be perfectly honest, no one knows for sure, and estimates will vary depending on who you talk to. My personal opinion (based on over 30 years of traveling into China, carrying Bibles, venturing into many remote villages, teaching among the unregistered house-church Christians, and, in more recent years, preaching by invitation in the "official" registered churches) is that the total Christians in China number approximately 80 to 90 million. This includes not only those who are members of the official, government-sanctioned, and registered Three-Self Church, but also the vastly more numerous Christians who are part of the unofficial and unregistered house-church movement, sometimes known as the "underground church."

One more question I hear frequently from Christians in the West is, "What about the persecution of Christians in China? How bad is it, really?" The general perception among Christians in the West is that the persecution of Christians in China is widespread, ongoing, and severe. Paul Hattaway's recent biography of Chinese Christian Brother Yun, The Heavenly Man, while an excellent book overall, may have helped reinforce this Western misconception of widespread persecution of Christians in China.

Don't get me wrong; persecution does occur in China. The government of China is officially atheistic, and only those Christians who are part of the registered, government-regulated Three-Self Church have "legal" status as believers. Officially, the unregistered house-church movement is illegal, and therefore, the millions of Chinese Christians who are part of it are, officially, subject to arrest and prosecution. And sometimes it happens.

Contrary to the common Western perception, however, persecution of Christians in China is not systemic, or even particularly widespread. Because of the tremendous size of China, both in population and land area, central government oversight of the nation as a whole is extremely difficult. Regional and provincial administrators, therefore, have a large degree of autonomy in their own areas, although they are ultimately accountable to the leadership in Beijing. The frequency and severity of persecution of Christians varies from one region to the next, depending on the attitude and viewpoint of the regional leaders. Christians in one region may suffer severe repression and hardship, while those in another region are left completely alone. With regard to the central government in Beijing, whatever may have been the repressive policies and practices of the past, under Chairman Mao and that regime, the current Beijing government does not follow a policy of systemic, ongoing persecution of Chinese Christians.

This is a truth about China and Christianity in China that is rarely heard in the West. The rest of the world, and particularly the West, need to know the truth about what is happening in China. China is changing. God is at work in magnificent and wonderful ways, although many of His ways often are subtle, "behind the scenes," and therefore not immediately or readily visible. Many challenges remain, of course, and being a Christian in China still carries risks. However, the overall picture is not as bleak as many Westerners have assumed. There is much cause for hope, and new doors are opening all the time.

I hope that by now you know the answer to the question, "Why China?" Not only are there still millions of Chinese who need Christ, but China's growing worldwide influence—economically, intellectually, scientifically, and in virtually every other discipline—makes the nation a pivotal key to global evangelization. As just one example, Chinese Christians have connections and inroads for witnessing to Muslims that Western Christians do not. Chinese Christians do not carry the "stigma" that the West has planted in the minds of so many Muslims. When Muslims can see Christ presented in a non-Western context, they are much more receptive.

Perhaps the story I have shared in this book has fired up your excitement for China. I hope so, for that is my prayer. You may be asking, "What can I do? How can I become involved?"

You can pray. Prayer should always be the first option, and not the last resort. God is mightily at work in China, and He responds to the faithful prayers of His people. If you can do nothing else, pray for us.

You can give. Search your heart and ask the Lord to show you the level of financial contribution. You can purchase Bibles and send them for distribution. There are still millions of Chinese Christians who do not have a personal copy of the Word of God. Better yet, don't send the Bibles, but bring them yourself. Revival Christian Church routinely carries Bibles into China, and often takes with us Christian visitors from the West who have brought Bibles and who wish to see firsthand what God is doing there.

You can open yourself to the possibility that God may be calling you to China (or somewhere else). Don't sell yourself short by assuming that you don't have the knowledge or the experience or the "whatever" you think it takes; don't say, "I'm not good enough for God to use me in that way." I will emphasize again—Kathy and I are the most ordinary people in the world. You don't have to be anybody special; in fact, God specializes in using ordinary people. All you need is a willing heart, and an openness to being led by the Holy Spirit. Ask God to show you if He is calling you into missions. Don't assume that such a call necessarily means uprooting your life and planting yourself on foreign soil for the rest of your life as career missionaries, the way Kathy and I have. There is just as much a need for people who are committed to periodic, short-term mission trips. Let God show you where He wants to plug you in. China today is an open door, and many other parts of the world formerly closed to the Gospel are starting to open up as well. The door is open. The question is—Will you walk through?

NOTE TO THE READER

If you are interested in learning more about China, its people, and the activity of God there, as well as receiving information about Revival Christian Church and the ministry they have carried on in China since 1978, stay posted. All this and more will be addressed in much greater detail in a future book coming soon! Please visit our website: www.rcmi.ac

ABOUT THE AUTHOR

Pastor Dennis Balcombe received the call of God on his life at a young age and traveled to China at the age of 24. He has lived in Hong Kong for the past 42 years. God has greatly used him to bless and strengthen the Chinese church; a church that now has well over one hundred million believers. He speaks fluent Mandarin and Cantonese. He continues to minister to the Chinese and many others throughout Asia and the world. As the founder of Revival Chinese Ministries International, he is a sought after speaker globally. Dennis lives with his wife Kathy in Hong Kong. They have two children, Sharon and Michael and two grandchildren.

CONTACT DENNIS BALCOMBE

Hong Kong

Revival Christian Church

G/F., Kwai Fong Terrace
15 Kwai Yi Road
Kwai Chung, N.T.
Hong Kong

Website: www.rcmi.ac

Email: rcmihkg@rcchk.org

Tel: 852-23807272

USA

Revival Christian Church

3295 School Street
Oakland CA 94602
U.S.A.

Website: rcmi-usa.org

Email: rcmiusa@rcchk.org

Tel: 510-437-1147

For our offices in other parts of the world, please visit our website: **www.rcmi.ac** and click on "contact us – offices worldwide" icon.

eGenBooks

Generation Culture Transformation
Specializing in publishing for generation culture change

Visit us Online at:
www.egenco.com
www.egenbooks.com

Write to: eGen Co. LLC
824 Tallow Hill Road
Chambersburg, PA 17202 USA
Phone: 717-461-3436
Email: info@egenco.com

 facebook.com/egenbooks

 twitter.com/vishaljets

 youtube.com/egenpub

 egenco.com/blog